INSTANT POT COOKBOOK 2022

SUPER DELICIOUS DESSERT RECIPES TO MASTER YOUR INSTANT POT

JANE KROSS

Table of Contents

Superb Banana Dessert 10

Rhubarb Dessert 11

Plum Delight 12

Refreshing Fruits Dish 13

Dessert Stew 14

Original Fruits Dessert 15

Delicious Apples and Cinnamon 16

Crazy Delicious Pudding 17

Wonderful Berry Pudding 19

Winter Fruits Dessert 21

Different Dessert 22

Orange Dessert 23

Great Pumpkin Dessert 25

Delicious Baked Apples 27

Moist Pumpkin Brownie 29

Lemon Custard 31

Pumpkin Pudding 33

Easy Yogurt Custard 35

Zucchini Pudding 37

Delicious Pina Colada 38

Apple Caramel Cake	39
Apple Rice Pudding	40
Vegan Coconut Risotto Pudding	41
Vanilla Avocado Pudding	42
Vanilla Almond Risotto	44
Coconut Raspberry Curd	45
Simple Chocolate Mousse	47
The Best Tropical Dessert Ever	49
Crème with Almond and Chocolate	51
Cinnamon Flan	53
Yummy Upside-Down Cake	55
Extraordinary Chocolate Cheesecake	57
Old-School Cheesecake	59
Sweet and Sour Tale Cake	61
Lazy Sunday Cake	63
Keto Chocolate Brownies	65
Sweet Porridge with a Twist	67
Cheesecake Tropicana	68
Classic Holiday Custard	70
Blackberry Espresso Brownies	72
Sweet Porridge with Blueberries	74
Vanilla Berry Cupcakes	76
Mini Cheesecakes with Berries	78
Special Berry Crisp with Cinnamon	80

Yummy Fire Cheesecake	82
Classic Carrot Cake	84
Classic Brownie with Blackberry-Goat Cheese Swirl	86
Special Birthday Cake	89
Holiday Blueberry Pudding	91
Fluffy Strawberry Cake	93
Chocolate Cheesecake	96
Raspberry Compote	98
Chocolate Cream	100
Butter Pancakes	102
Lemon Cupcakes with Blueberries	104
Chocolate Brownies	106
Peach Pie	108
Almond Butter Cookies	110
Mini Brownie Cakes	112
Egg Salad	114
Granny's Cheesy Soup	116
Cheesy Spicy Eggs	118
Savory Egg Custard	120
Indian Style Egg Muffins	122
Bell Pepper and Egg "Sandwich"	123
Cheese, Sausage and Vegetable Bake	125
Avocado, Goat Cheese and Egg Muffins	127
Avocado Boats - Spicy and Stuffed	129

Cheesy Beer Dip	131
Healthy Breakfast Wraps	133
Keto Cheesy Pizza	134
Peppery Habanero Eggs	136
Egg Salad with Mustard Seed Dressing	138
Egg Salad Bowl	140
Casserole with Asparagus and Cheese	142
Festive Breakfast Eggs	144
Green Dip with Cheese and Mustard	145
Cheesy Cauliflower Dip	146
The Best Keto Breakfast	148
Yummy Keto Wraps	150
Sausage and Tomatoes Stew	152
Rosemary Beef and Parsnips Stew	153
Italian Chicken and Spinach Stew	154
Chicken and Okra Stew	155
Peas and Turkey Stew	157
Turkey and Brussels Sprouts Stew	159
Lamb and Peppers Stew	161
Cinnamon Pork Stew	162
Pesto Pork Stew	163
Beef and Turnips Stew	164
Oregano Lamb and Tomatoes Stew	165
Chili Beef Stew	166

Lemon Kale and Chicken Stew 167

Tarragon Beef Stew 168

Bacon and Spinach Stew 169

Shrimp and Cod Stew 170

Green Beans and Chicken Stew 171

Turmeric Quinoa and Chicken Stew 172

Light Lunch Soup 174

North-American Veggie Soup 176

Bolognese Soup 178

Ham and Asparagus Soup 180

A Different Wedding Soup 182

Oxtail Soup 184

Taco Soup 186

Minestrone Soup 188

Coconut Tomato Soup 190

Creamy Chicken Soup 192

Ham and Bean Soup 194

Chicken Mushroom Soup 196

Chicken Kale Soup 198

Italian Sausage Kale Soup 200

Chickpea Soup with Greens 202

Cheesy Meatball Soup 204

Clam Chowder 207

Sausage Bacon and Mushroom Chowder 209

Turkey and Daikon Chowder 211
Pork and Vegetable Stock Recipe 213
Chicken Stock Recipe 215

Superb Banana Dessert

Preparation time: 10 minutes

Cooking time: 30 minutes

Servings: 4

Ingredients:

- Juice from ½ lemon
- 2 tablespoons stevia
- 3 ounces water
- 1 tablespoon coconut oil
- 4 bananas, peeled and sliced
- ½ teaspoon cardamom seeds

Directions:

1. Put bananas, stevia, water, oil, lemon juice and cardamom in your instant pot, stir a bit, cover and cook on High for 30 minutes, shaking the pot from time to time.
2. Divide into bowls and serve.
3. Enjoy!

Nutritional Values per serving: Calories 87, fat 1, fiber 2, carbs 3, protein 3

Rhubarb Dessert

Preparation time: 10 minutes

Cooking time: 5 minutes

Servings: 4

Ingredients:

- 5 cups rhubarb, chopped
- 2 tablespoons ghee, melted
- 1/3 cup water
- 1 tablespoon stevia
- 1 teaspoon vanilla extract

Directions:

1. Put rhubarb, ghee, water, stevia and vanilla extract in your instant pot, cover and cook on High for 5 minutes.
2. Divide into small bowls and serve cold.
3. Enjoy!

Nutritional Values per serving: Calories 83, fat 2, fiber 1, carbs 2, protein 2

Plum Delight

Preparation time: 10 minutes

Cooking time: 5 minutes

Servings: 10

Ingredients:

- 4 pounds plums, stones removed and chopped
- 1 cup water
- 2 tablespoons stevia
- 1 teaspoon cinnamon, powder
- ½ teaspoon cardamom, ground

Directions:

1. Put plums, water, stevia, cinnamon and cardamom in your instant pot, cover and cook on High for 5 minutes.
2. Stir well, pulse a bit using an immersion blender, divide into small jars and serve.
3. Enjoy!

Nutritional Values per serving: Calories 83, fat 0, fiber 1, carbs 2, protein 5

Refreshing Fruits Dish

Preparation time: 10 minutes

Cooking time: 10 minutes

Servings: 4

Ingredients:

- 1 and ½ pounds plums, stones removed and halved
- 2 tablespoons stevia
- 1 tablespoon cinnamon powder
- 2 apples, cored, peeled and cut into wedges
- 2 tablespoons lemon zest, grated
- 2 teaspoons balsamic vinegar
- 1 cup hot water

Directions:

- Put plums, water, apples, stevia, cinnamon, lemon zest and vinegar in your instant pot, cover and cook on High for 10 minutes.
- Stir again well, divide into small cups and serve cold.

Nutritional Values per serving: Calories 73, fat 0, fiber 1, carbs 2, protein 4

Dessert Stew

Preparation time: 10 minutes

Cooking time: 6 minutes

Servings: 6

Ingredients:

- 14 plums, stones removed and halved
- 2 tablespoons stevia
- 1 teaspoon cinnamon powder
- ¼ cup water
- 2 tablespoons arrowroot powder

Directions:

1. Put plums, stevia, cinnamon, water and arrowroot in your instant pot, cover and cook on High for 6 minutes.
2. Divide into small jars and serve cold.
3. Enjoy!

Nutritional Values per serving: Calories 83, fat 0, fiber 1, carbs 2, protein 2

Original Fruits Dessert

Preparation time: 10 minutes

Cooking time: 10 minutes

Servings: 10

Ingredients:

- 3 cups canned pineapple chunks, drained
- 3 cups canned cherries, drained
- 2 cups canned apricots, halved and drained
- 2 cups canned peach slices, drained
- 3 cups natural applesauce
- 2 cups canned mandarin oranges, drained
- 2 tablespoons stevia
- 1 teaspoon cinnamon powder

Directions:

1. Put pineapples, cherries, apricots, peaches, applesauce, oranges, cinnamon and stevia in your instant pot, cover and cook on High for 10 minutes.
2. Divide into small bowls and serve cold.
3. Enjoy!

Nutritional Values per serving: Calories 120, fat 1, fiber 2, carbs 3, protein 2

Delicious Apples and Cinnamon

Preparation time: 10 minutes

Cooking time: 10 minutes

Servings: 8

Ingredients:

- 1 teaspoon cinnamon powder
- 12 ounces apples, cored and chopped
- 2 tablespoons flax seed meal mixed with 1 tablespoon water
- ½ cup coconut cream
- 3 tablespoons stevia
- ½ teaspoon nutmeg
- 2 teaspoons vanilla extract
- 1/3 cup pecans, chopped

Directions:

1. In your instant pot, mix flax seed meal with coconut cream, vanilla, nutmeg, stevia, apples and cinnamon, stir a bit, cover and cook on High for 10 minutes.
2. Divide into bowls, sprinkle pecans on top and serve.
3. Enjoy!

Nutritional Values per serving: Calories 120, fat 3, fiber 2, carbs 3, protein 3

Crazy Delicious Pudding

Preparation time: 10 minutes

Cooking time: 35 minutes

Servings: 6

Ingredients:

- 1 mandarin, sliced
- Juice from 2 mandarins
- 3 tablespoons stevia
- 4 ounces ghee, melted
- ½ cup water
- 2 tablespoons flax meal
- ¾ cup coconut flour
- 1 teaspoon baking powder
- ¾ cup almonds, ground

- Olive oil cooking spray

Directions:

1. Grease a loaf pan, arrange sliced mandarin on the bottom and leave aside.
2. In a bowl, mix ghee with stevia, flax meal, almonds, mandarin juice, flour and baking powder, stir and spread this over mandarin slices.
3. Add the water to your instant pot, place the trivet on top, add loaf pan, cover and cook on High for 35 minutes.
4. Leave aside to cool down, slice and serve.
5. Enjoy!

Nutritional Values per serving: Calories 200, fat 2, fiber 2, carbs 3, protein 4

Wonderful Berry Pudding

Preparation time: 10 minutes

Cooking time: 35 minutes

Servings: 6

Ingredients:

- 1 cup almond flour
- 2 tablespoons lemon juice
- 2 cups blueberries
- 2 teaspoons baking powder
- ½ teaspoon nutmeg, ground
- ½ cup coconut milk
- 3 tablespoons stevia
- 1 tablespoon flax meal mixed with 1 tablespoon water
- 3 tablespoons ghee, melted
- 1 teaspoon vanilla extract
- 1 tablespoon arrowroot powder
- 1 cup cold water

Directions:

- In a greased heat proof dish, mix blueberries and lemon juice, toss a bit and spread on the bottom.
- In a bowl, mix flour with nutmeg, stevia, baking powder, vanilla, ghee, flaxseed meal, arrowroot and milk, stir well again and spread over blueberries.
- Put the water in your instant pot, add the trivet, and the heatproof dish, cover and cook on High for 35 minutes.
- Leave pudding to cool down, transfer to dessert bowls and serve.
- Enjoy!

Nutritional Values per serving: Calories 220, fat 4, fiber 4, carbs 9, protein 6

Winter Fruits Dessert

Preparation time: 10 minutes

Cooking time: 15 minutes

Servings: 6

Ingredients:

- 1-quart water
- 2 tablespoons stevia
- 1 pound mixed apples, pears and cranberries
- 5-star anise
- A pinch of cloves, ground
- 2 cinnamon sticks
- Zest from 1 orange, grated
- Zest from 1 lemon, grated

Directions:

1. Put the water, stevia, apples, pears, cranberries, star anise, cinnamon, orange and lemon zest and cloves in your instant pot, cover and cook on High for 15 minutes.
2. Serve cold.
3. Enjoy!

Nutritional Values per serving: Calories 98, fat 0, fiber 0, carbs 0, protein 2

Different Dessert

Preparation time: 10 minutes

Cooking time: 4 minutes

Servings: 2

Ingredients:

- 2 cups orange juice
- 4 pears, peeled, cored and cut into medium chunks
- 5 cardamom pods
- 2 tablespoons stevia
- 1 cinnamon stick
- 1 small ginger piece, grated

Directions:

1. Place pears, cardamom, orange juice, stevia, cinnamon and ginger in your instant pot, cover and cook on High for 4 minutes.
2. Divide into small bowls and serve cold.
3. Enjoy!

Nutritional Values per serving: Calories 100, fat 0, fiber 1, carbs 1, protein 2

Orange Dessert

Preparation time: 10 minutes

Cooking time: 30 minutes

Servings: 4

Ingredients:

- 1 and ¾ cup water
- 1 teaspoon baking powder
- 1 cup coconut flour
- 2 tablespoons stevia
- ½ teaspoon cinnamon powder
- 3 tablespoons coconut oil, melted
- ½ cup coconut milk
- ½ cup pecans, chopped
- ½ cup raisins
- ½ cup orange peel, grated
- ¾ cup orange juice

Directions:

1. In a bowl, mix flour with stevia, baking powder, cinnamon, 2 tablespoons oil, milk, pecans and raisins, stir and transfer to a greased heat proof dish.
2. Heat up a small pan over medium high heat, mix ¾ cup water with orange juice, orange peel and the rest of the oil, stir, bring to a boil and pour over the pecans mix.
3. Put 1 cup water in your instant pot, add the trivet, add heat proof dish, cover and cook on High for 30 minutes.
4. Serve cold.
5. Enjoy!

Nutritional Values per serving: Calories 142, fat 3, fiber 1, carbs 3, protein 3

Great Pumpkin Dessert

Preparation time: 10 minutes

Cooking time: 30 minutes

Servings: 10

Ingredients:

- 1 and ½ teaspoons baking powder
- 2 cups coconut flour
- ½ teaspoon baking soda
- ¼ teaspoon nutmeg, ground
- 1 teaspoons cinnamon powder
- ¼ teaspoon ginger, grated
- 1 tablespoon coconut oil, melted
- 1 egg white
- 1 tablespoon vanilla extract
- 1 cup pumpkin puree
- 2 tablespoons stevia
- 1 teaspoon lemon juice
- 1 cup water

Directions:

1. In a bowl, flour with baking powder, baking soda, cinnamon, ginger, nutmeg, oil, egg white, ghee, vanilla extract, pumpkin puree, stevia and lemon juice, stir well and transfer this to a greased cake pan.
2. Put the water in your instant pot, add trivet, add cake pan, cover and cook on High for 30 minutes.
3. Leave cake to cool down, slice and serve.
4. Enjoy!

Nutritional Values per serving: Calories 180, fat 3, fiber 2, carbs 3, protein 4

Delicious Baked Apples

Servings: 6

Cooking Time: 14 minutes

Ingredients:

- 6 apples, cored and cut into wedges
- ¼ tsp nutmeg
- 1 tsp cinnamon
- 1/3 cup honey
- 1 cup red wine
- ¼ cup pecans, chopped
- ¼ cup raisins

Directions:

1. Add all ingredients into the instant pot and stir well.
2. Seal pot with lid and cook on manual mode for 4 minutes.
3. Allow to release pressure naturally for 10 minutes then release using quick release method.
4. Stir well and serve.

Nutritional Values per serving:

Calories: 233; Carbohydrates: 52.7g; Protein: 1g; Fat: 1.3g; Sugar: 42.6g; Sodium: 5mg

Moist Pumpkin Brownie

Servings: 16

Cooking Time: 40 minutes

Ingredients:

- 3 eggs
- 1 tsp pumpkin pie spice
- ¾ cup cocoa powder
- ¼ cup palm sugar
- ¼ cup maple syrup
- ½ cup pumpkin puree
- ¼ cup coconut oil
- Pinch of salt

Directions:
1. Spray baking dish with cooking spray and set aside.
2. Add all ingredients into the large bowl and stir well to combine. Pour batter into the prepared baking dish.
3. Pour 1 cup of water into the instant pot than place trivet in the pot.
4. Place baking dish on top of the trivet.
5. Seal pot with lid and cook on high for 4o minutes.
6. Release pressure using quick release method than open the lid.
7. Remove dish from the pot and set aside to cool completely.
8. Cut into pieces and serve.

Nutritional Values per serving:

Calories: 77; Carbohydrates: 9.3g; Protein: 1.9g; Fat: 4.8g; Sugar: 5.6g; Sodium: 32mg

Lemon Custard

Servings: 4

Cooking Time: 11 minutes

Ingredients:

- 4 eggs
- 1 tsp lemon extract
- 2/3 cup sugar
- 2 tsp lemon zest
- 2 ½ cups milk

Directions:

1. In a saucepan, add lemon zest and milk and heat over medium heat. Bring to boil and stir constantly.
2. Once milk starts to boil up then remove from heat. Set aside to cool for 15 minutes.
3. Pour milk through a strainer into a bowl.
4. In another bowl beat together eggs, lemon extract for 2-3 minutes.
5. Slowly pour milk to the egg mixture and mix until smooth and creamy.
6. Pour mixture into the 4 ramekins and cover each with foil.
7. Pour 2 cups of water into the instant pot than place trivet in the pot.

8. Place ramekins on top of the trivet.
9. Seal pot with lid and cook on high for 8 minutes.
10. Release pressure using quick release method than open the lid.
11. Remove ramekins from the pot and set aside to cool completely.
12. Place custard ramekins in the refrigerator for 2 hours.
13. Serve chilled and enjoy.

Nutritional Values per serving:

Calories: 268; Carbohydrates: 41.5g; Protein: 10.6g; Fat: 7.5g; Sugar: 40.7g; Sodium: 134mg

Pumpkin Pudding

Servings: 4

Cooking Time: 14 minutes

Ingredients:

- 4 cups pumpkin, cubed
- 1 tbsp raisins
- ½ tsp cardamom powder
- ½ cup desiccated coconut
- 10 tbsp brown sugar
- ½ cup almond milk
- 2 tbsp ghee

Directions:

1. Add ghee into the instant pot and set the pot on sauté mode.
2. Add pumpkin and sauté for 2-3 minutes. Add almond milk and stir well.
3. Seal pot with lid and cook on high for 5 minutes.
4. Release pressure using quick release method than open the lid.
5. Mash the pumpkin using the potato masher.
6. Add sugar and cook on sauté mode for 2-3 minutes.
7. Add remaining ingredients and stir well to combine and cook for 2-3 minutes.
8. Serve warm and enjoy.

Nutritional Values per serving:

Calories: 301; Carbohydrates: 14.2g; Protein: 3.5g; Fat: 14.2g; Sugar: 32.3g; Sodium: 23mg

Easy Yogurt Custard

Servings: 6

Cooking Time: 40 minutes

Ingredients:

- 1 cup Greek yogurt
- 2 tsp cardamom powder
- 1 cup milk
- 1 cup condensed milk

Directions:

1. Add all ingredients into the heat-safe bowl and mix until well combined. Cover bowl with foil.
2. Pour 2 cups of water into the instant pot than place trivet in the pot.
3. Place bowl on top of the trivet. Seal pot with lid and cook on high for 20 minutes.
4. Allow to release pressure naturally for 20 minutes then release using quick release method.
5. Remove bowl from the pot and set aside to cool completely.
6. Place custard bowl in refrigerator for 1 hour.
7. Serve chilled and enjoy.

Nutritional Values per serving:

Calories: 215; Carbohydrates: 33.1g; Protein: 7.8g; Fat: 5.8g; Sugar: 32.4g; Sodium: 113mg

Zucchini Pudding

Servings: 4

Cooking Time: 20 minutes

Ingredients:

- 2 cups zucchini, shredded
- ½ tsp cardamom powder
- 1/3 cup sugar
- 5 oz half and half
- 5 oz milk

Directions:

1. Add all ingredients except cardamom to the instant pot and stir well.
2. Seal pot with lid and cook on high for 10 minutes.
3. Allow to release pressure naturally for 10 minutes then release using quick release method.
4. Add cardamom and stir well.
5. Serve and enjoy.

Nutritional Values per serving:

Calories: 136; Carbohydrates: 22g; Protein: 2.9g; Fat: 4.9g; Sugar: 19.3g; Sodium: 37mg

Delicious Pina Colada

Servings: 8

Cooking Time: 12 minutes

Ingredients:

- 1 cup Arborio rice
- 1 tbsp cinnamon
- 5 oz can pineapple, crushed
- oz coconut milk
- 1 cup condensed milk
- 1 ½ cups water

Directions:

1. Add rice and water into the instant pot and stir well.
2. Seal pot with lid and cook on low for 12 minutes.
3. Release pressure using quick release method than open the lid.
4. Add remaining ingredients and stir well.
5. Serve and enjoy.

Nutritional Values per serving:

Calories: 330; Carbohydrates: 45.4g; Protein: 5.8g; Fat: 14.9g; Sugar: 24.2g; Sodium: 59mg

Apple Caramel Cake

Servings: 8

Cooking Time: 35 minutes

Ingredients:

- 21 oz apple fruit filling
- ¼ cup caramel syrup
- ½ cup butter, cut into slices
- 15 oz yellow cake mix

Directions:

1. Spray baking dish with cooking spray. Spread apple fruit filling in the bottom of baking dish.
2. Add caramel syrup and stir to coat.
3. Top with yellow cake mix and butter slices.
4. Pour 1 cup of water into the instant pot than place trivet in the pot.
5. Place baking dish on top of the trivet.
6. Seal pot with lid and cook on high for 35 minutes.
7. Release pressure using quick release method than open the lid.
8. Serve and enjoy.

Nutritional Values per serving:

Calories: 357; Carbohydrates: 57g; Protein: 2g; Fat: 13g; Sugar: 28g; Sodium: 596mg

Apple Rice Pudding

Servings: 8

Cooking Time: 15 minutes

Ingredients:

- ¾ cup Arborio rice
- 1 tsp cinnamon
- 1 cinnamon stick
- 1 tsp vanilla
- ¼ apple, peeled and chopped
- 2 rhubarb stalks, chopped
- ½ cup water
- 1 ½ cup milk

Directions:

1. Add all ingredients into the instant pot and stir well.
2. Seal pot with lid and cook on manual mode for 15 minutes.
3. Release pressure using quick release method than open the lid.
4. Stir well and serve.

Nutritional Values per serving:

Calories: 96; Carbohydrates: 18.3g; Protein: 2.8g; Fat: 1.1g; Sugar: 3g; Sodium: 24mg

Vegan Coconut Risotto Pudding

Servings: 6

Cooking Time: 30 minutes

Ingredients:

- ¾ cup Arborio rice
- ¼ cup maple syrup
- 1 ½ cups water
- ½ cup shredded coconut
- 1 tsp lemon juice
- ½ tsp vanilla
- 15 oz can coconut milk

Directions:

1. Add all ingredients into the instant pot and stir well.
2. Seal pot with lid and cook on manual mode for 20 minutes.
3. Allow to release pressure naturally for 10 minutes then release using quick release method.
4. Stir well and using blender blend pudding until smooth.
5. Serve and enjoy.

Nutritional Values per serving:

Calories: 284; Carbohydrates: 30.8g; Protein: 3.3g; Fat: 17.5g; Sugar: 8.3g; Sodium: 15mg

Vanilla Avocado Pudding

Servings: 2

Cooking Time: 3 minutes

Ingredients:

- 1/2 avocado, cut into cubes
- 1 tsp agar powder
- 1/4 cup coconut cream
- 1 cup coconut milk
- 2 tsp swerve
- 1 tsp vanilla

Directions:

1. Add coconut cream and avocado into the blender and blend until smooth. Set aside.
2. In a large bowl, whisk together coconut milk, vanilla, swerve, and agar powder. Stir until well combined.
3. Add coconut cream and avocado mixture and stir well.
4. Pour mixture into a heat-safe bowl.
5. Pour one cup of water into the instant pot then place a trivet in the pot.
6. Place bowl on top of the trivet.
7. Seal pot with lid and cook on steam mode for 3 minutes.

8. Release pressure using quick release method than open the lid.
9. Remove bowl from the pot and set aside to cool completely.
10. Place bowl in refrigerator for 1 hour.
11. Serve and enjoy.

Nutritional Values per serving:

Calories: 308; Carbohydrates: 27.9g; Protein: 2.1g; Fat: 21.8g; Sugar: 19.6g; Sodium: 32mg

Vanilla Almond Risotto

Servings: 4

Cooking Time: 15 minutes

Ingredients:

- 1 cup Arborio rice
- 1 cup coconut milk
- 2 cups unsweetened almond milk
- 1/4 cup sliced almonds
- 2 tsp vanilla extract
- 1/3 cup sugar

Directions:

1. Add almonds and coconut milk into the instant pot and stir well.
2. Seal pot with lid and cook on high for 5 minutes.
3. Allow to release pressure naturally for 10 minutes then release using quick release method.
4. Stir in vanilla extract and sweetener.
5. Serve and enjoy.

Nutritional Values per serving:

Calories: 432; Carbohydrates: 60.3g; Protein: 6.3g; Fat: 19.3g; Sugar: 19.2g; Sodium: 102mg

Coconut Raspberry Curd

Preparation Time: 20 minutes + chilling time

Servings 4

Nutritional Values per serving: 334 Calories; 32.9g Fat; 6.6g Total Carbs; 2.9g Protein; 3.6g Sugars

Ingredients

- 4 ounces coconut oil, softened
- 3/4 cup Swerve
- 4 egg yolks, beaten
- 1/2 cup blueberries
- 1 teaspoon grated lemon zest
- 1/2 teaspoon vanilla extract
- 1/2 teaspoon star anise, ground

Directions

1. Blend the coconut oil and Swerve in a food processor.
2. Gradually mix in the eggs; continue to blend for 1 minute longer.
3. Now, add blueberries, lemon zest, vanilla, and star anise. Divide the mixture among four Mason jars and cover them with lids.
4. Add 1 ½ cups of water and a metal rack to the Instant Pot. Now, lower your jars onto the rack.

5. Secure the lid. Choose "Manual" mode and High pressure; cook for 15 minutes. Once cooking is complete, use a natural pressure release; carefully remove the lid. Serve
6. Place in your refrigerator until ready to serve. Bon appétit!

Simple Chocolate Mousse

Preparation Time: 20 minutes + chilling time

Servings 6

Nutritional Values per serving: 205 Calories; 18.3g Fat; 5.2g Total Carbs; 3.2g Protein; 2.6g Sugars

Ingredients

- 1 cup full-fat milk
- 1 cup heavy cream
- 4 egg yolks, beaten
- 1/3 cup sugar
- 1/4 teaspoon grated nutmeg
- 1/4 teaspoon ground cinnamon
- 1/4 cup unsweetened cocoa powder

Directions

1. In a small pan, bring the milk and cream to a simmer.
2. In a mixing dish, thoroughly combine the remaining ingredients. Add this egg mixture to the warm milk mixture.
3. Pour the mixture into ramekins.
4. Add 1 ½ cups of water and a metal rack to the Instant Pot. Now, lower your ramekins onto the rack.
5. Secure the lid. Choose "Manual" mode and High pressure; cook for 10 minutes. Once cooking is complete, use a natural pressure release; carefully remove the lid. Serve
6. Serve well chilled and enjoy!

The Best Tropical Dessert Ever

Preparation Time: 15 minutes + chilling time

Servings 4

Nutritional Values per serving: 118 Calories; 8.2g Fat; 6.6g Total Carbs; 3.7g Protein; 2.6g Sugars

Ingredients

- 3 egg yolks, well whisked
- 1/3 cup Swerve
- 1/4 cup water
- 3 tablespoons cacao powder, unsweetened
- 3/4 cup whipping cream
- 1/3 cup coconut milk
- 1/4 cup shredded coconut
- 1 teaspoon vanilla essence
- A pinch of grated nutmeg
- A pinch of salt

Directions

1. Place the egg in a mixing bowl.
2. In a pan, heat the Swerve, water and cacao powder and whisk well to combine.
3. Now, stir in the whipping cream and milk; cook until heated through. Add shredded coconut, vanilla, nutmeg, and salt.
4. Now, slowly and gradually pour the chocolate mixture into the bowl with egg yolks. Stir to combine well and pour into ramekins.
5. Add 1 ½ cups of water and a metal rack to the Instant Pot. Now, lower your ramekins onto the rack.
6. Secure the lid. Choose "Manual" mode and High pressure; cook for 8 minutes. Once cooking is complete, use a quick pressure release; carefully remove the lid.
7. Place in your refrigerator until ready to serve. Bon appétit!

Crème with Almond and Chocolate

Preparation Time: 15 minutes

Servings 4

Nutritional Values per serving: 401 Calories; 37.1g Fat; 5.2g Total Carbs; 9.1g Protein; 1.7g Sugars

Ingredients

- 2 cups heavy whipping cream
- 1/2 cup water
- 4 eggs
- 1/3 cup Swerve
- 1 teaspoon almond extract
- 1 teaspoon vanilla extract
- 1/3 cup almonds, ground
- 2 tablespoons coconut oil, room temperature
- 4 tablespoons cacao powder
- 2 tablespoons gelatin

Directions

1. Start by adding 1 ½ cups of water and a metal rack to your Instant Pot.
2. Blend the cream, water, eggs, Swerve, almond extract, vanilla extract and almonds in your food processor.
3. Add the remaining ingredients and process for a minute longer.
4. Divide the mixture between four Mason jars; cover your jars with lids. Lower the jars onto the rack.
5. Secure the lid. Choose "Manual" mode and High pressure; cook for 7 minutes. Once cooking is complete, use a natural pressure release; carefully remove the lid. Bon appétit!

Cinnamon Flan

Preparation Time: 15 minutes

Servings 6

Nutritional Values per serving: 263 Calories; 21.2g Fat; 3.2g Total Carbs; 10.5g Protein; 2.8g Sugars

Ingredients

- 6 eggs
- 1 cup Swerve
- 1 ½ cups double cream
- 1/2 cup water
- 3 tablespoons dark rum
- A pinch of salt
- A pinch of freshly grated nutmeg
- 1/4 teaspoon ground cinnamon
- 1 teaspoon vanilla extract

Directions

1. Start by adding 1 ½ cups of water and a metal rack to your Instant Pot.
2. In a mixing bowl, thoroughly combine eggs and Swerve. Add double cream, water, rum, salt, nutmeg, cinnamon, and vanilla extract.
3. Pour mixture into a baking dish. Lower the dish onto the rack.
4. Secure the lid. Choose "Manual" mode and High pressure; cook for 10 minutes. Once cooking is complete, use a natural pressure release; carefully remove the lid.
5. Serve well chilled and enjoy!

Yummy Upside-Down Cake

Preparation Time: 35 minutes

Servings 5

Nutritional Values per serving: 193 Calories; 17.9g Fat; 5.1g Total Carbs; 1.2g Protein; 2.4g Sugars

Ingredients

- 1/2 pound raspberries
- 1 ½ tablespoons lemon juice
- 1 cup coconut flour
- 2 tablespoons cassava flour
- 1/2 teaspoon baking powder
- 1/8 teaspoon sea salt
- 1/4 cup coconut oil, melted
- 1 tablespoon monk fruit powder
- 1/2 teaspoon ground cinnamon
- 1/4 teaspoon grated nutmeg
- 1/2 teaspoon orange zest
- 1 teaspoon vanilla paste
- 1 ½ teaspoons powdered agar

Directions

1. Add 1 ½ cups water and a metal rack to the Instant Pot.
2. In a mixing bowl, thoroughly combine raspberries and lemon juice. Spread raspberries in the bottom of the pan.
3. In another mixing bowl, thoroughly combine coconut flour, cassava flour, baking powder, and sea salt.
4. In the third bowl, mix the coconut oil, monk fruit powder, cinnamon, nutmeg, orange zest, and vanilla. Add powdered agar and mix until everything is well incorporated.
5. Pour the liquid ingredients over dry ingredients and mix to form a dough; flatten it to form a circle.
6. Place this dough in a baking pan and cover the raspberries. Cover the pan with a sheet of aluminum foil.
7. Lower the pan onto the metal rack.
8. Secure the lid. Choose "Manual" mode and High pressure; cook for 27 minutes. Once cooking is complete, use a natural pressure release; carefully remove the lid.
9. Finally, turn the cake pan upside down and unmold it on a platter. Enjoy!

Extraordinary Chocolate Cheesecake

Preparation Time: 25 minutes + chilling time

Servings 10

Nutritional Values per serving: 351 Calories; 35.6g Fat; 4.8g Total Carbs; 4.3g Protein; 1.7g Sugars

Ingredients

- Crust:
- 1/3 cup coconut flour
- 1/3 cup almond flour
- 2 tablespoons arrowroot flour
- 2 tablespoons cocoa powder, unsweetened
- 2 tablespoons monk fruit powder
- 1/4 cup coconut oil, melted
- Filling:
- 10 ounces cream cheese, softened
- 8 ounces heavy cream, softened
- 1 teaspoon monk fruit powder
- 1/2 cup cocoa powder, unsweetened
- 3 eggs yolks, at room temperature
- 1/3 cup sour cream
- 4 ounces butter, melted
- 1/2 teaspoon vanilla essence

Directions

1. Prepare your Instant Pot by adding 1 ½ cups of water and a metal rack to its bottom.
2. Coat a bottom of a baking pan with a piece of parchment paper.
3. In mixing bowl, combine coconut flour, almond flour, arrowroot powder, 2 tablespoons of cocoa powder, and 2 tablespoons of monk fruit powder; now, stir in melted coconut oil.
4. Press the crust mixture into the bottom of the prepared baking pan.
5. To make the filling, mix the cream cheese, heavy cream, monk fruit powder, and cocoa powder.
6. Now, fold in the eggs, sour cream, butter, and vanilla; continue to blend until everything is well incorporated,
7. Lower the baking pan onto the rack. Cover with a sheet of foil, making a foil sling.
8. Secure the lid. Choose "Manual" mode and High pressure; cook for 18 minutes. Once cooking is complete, use a natural pressure release; carefully remove the lid.
9. Place this cheesecake in your refrigerator for 3 to 4 hours. Bon appétit!

Old-School Cheesecake

Preparation Time: 35 minutes + chilling time

Servings 10

Nutritional Values per serving: 188 Calories; 17.2g Fat; 4.5g Total Carbs; 5.5g Protein; 1.3g Sugars

Ingredients

- Crust:
- 1/2 cup almond flour
- 1/2 cup coconut flour
- 1 ½ tablespoons powdered erythritol
- 1/4 teaspoon kosher salt
- 3 tablespoons butter, melted
- Filling:
- 8 ounces sour cream, at room temperature
- 8 ounces cream cheese, at room temperature
- 1/2 cup powdered erythritol
- 3 tablespoons orange juice
- 1/2 teaspoon ginger powder
- 1 teaspoon vanilla extract
- 3 eggs, at room temperature

Directions

1. Line a round baking pan with a piece of parchment paper.
2. In a mixing bowl, thoroughly combine all crust ingredients in the order listed above.
3. Press the crust mixture into the bottom of the pan.
4. Then, make the filling by mixing the sour cream and cream cheese until uniform and smooth; add the remaining ingredients and continue to beat until everything is well combined.
5. Pour the cream cheese mixture over the crust. Cover with aluminum foil, making a foil sling.
6. Place 1 ½ cups of water and a metal trivet in your Instant Pot. Then, place the pan on the metal rack.
7. Secure the lid. Choose "Manual" mode and High pressure; cook for 30 minutes. Once cooking is complete, use a natural pressure release; carefully remove the lid. Serve well chilled and enjoy!

Sweet and Sour Tale Cake

Preparation Time: 25 minutes

Servings 6

Nutritional Values per serving: 173 Calories; 15.6g Fat; 2.5g Total Carbs; 6.2g Protein; 1.6g Sugars

Ingredients

- Crust:
- 3/4 cup coconut flour
- 1/4 cup coconut oil
- 2 tablespoons Swerve
- 1/2 teaspoon pure lemon extract
- 1/2 teaspoon pure coconut extract
- 1/2 teaspoon pure vanilla extract
- 1/2 teaspoon baking powder
- A pinch of grated nutmeg
- A pinch of salt
- Filling:
- 4 eggs
- 1/2 cup Swerve
- 3 tablespoons freshly squeezed lemon juice
- 3 tablespoons shredded coconut
- 1/4 teaspoon cinnamon powder

Directions

1. Start by adding 1 ½ cups of water and a metal rack to your Instant Pot. Now, spritz a baking pan with a nonstick cooking spray (butter flavor.
2. Then, thoroughly combine all crust ingredients in your food processor. Now, spread the crust mixture evenly on the bottom of the prepared pan. Do not forget to prick a few holes with a fork.
3. Lower the baking pan onto the rack.
4. Secure the lid. Choose "Manual" mode and High pressure; cook for 8 minutes. Once cooking is complete, use a quick pressure release; carefully remove the lid.
5. Meanwhile, thoroughly combine all filling ingredients in your food processor. Spread the filling mixture evenly over top of the warm crust.
6. Return to the Instant Pot.
7. Secure the lid. Choose "Manual" mode and High pressure; cook for 15 minutes. Once cooking is complete, use a quick pressure release; carefully remove the lid.
8. Cut into squares and serve at room temperature or chilled. Bon appétit!

Lazy Sunday Cake

Preparation Time: 30 minutes

Servings 6

Nutritional Values per serving: 121 Calories; 7.3g Fat; 5.9g Total Carbs; 6.5g Protein; 2.3g Sugars

Ingredients

- 1/2 cup peanut butter
- 1 pound zucchini, shredded
- 1/4 cup Swerve
- 2 eggs, beaten
- 1/2 teaspoon ground star anise
- 1 teaspoon ground cinnamon
- 1/4 teaspoon grated nutmeg
- 1/2 teaspoon rum extract
- 1/2 teaspoon vanilla
- 1/2 teaspoon baking powder

Directions

1. Start by adding 1 ½ cups of water and a metal trivet to your Instant Pot. Now, spritz a baking pan with a nonstick cooking spray.
2. In a mixing dish, thoroughly combine all ingredients until uniform, creamy and smooth. Pour the batter into the prepared pan.
3. Lower the pan onto the trivet.
4. Secure the lid. Choose "Bean/Chili" mode and High pressure; cook for 25 minutes. Once cooking is complete, use a natural pressure release; carefully remove the lid.
5. Allow your cake to cool completely before cutting and serving. Bon appétit!

Keto Chocolate Brownies

Preparation Time: 30 minutes

Servings 6

Nutritional Values per serving: 384 Calories; 36.6g Fat; 5.2g Total Carbs; 7.7g Protein; 1.3g Sugars

Ingredients

- 4 ounces chocolate, sugar-free
- 1/2 cup coconut oil
- 2 cups Swerve
- 4 eggs, whisked
- 1 teaspoon vanilla paste
- 1/4 teaspoon sea salt
- 1/4 teaspoon grated nutmeg
- 1/2 teaspoon dried lavender flowers
- 1/4 cup almond flour
- 1/2 cup whipped cream

Directions

1. Start by adding 1 ½ cups of water and a metal trivet to your Instant Pot. Now, spritz a baking pan with a nonstick cooking spray.
2. Thoroughly combine the chocolate, coconut oil, and Swerve. Gradually, whisk in the eggs. Add the vanilla paste, salt, nutmeg, lavender flowers and almond flour; mix until everything is well incorporated.
3. Secure the lid. Choose "Bean/Chili" mode and High pressure; cook for 25 minutes. Once cooking is complete, use a natural pressure release; carefully remove the lid.
4. Top with whipped cream and serve well chilled. Bon appétit!

Sweet Porridge with a Twist

Preparation Time: 10 minutes

Servings 2

Nutritional Values per serving: 363 Calories; 36.4g Fat; 6.2g Total Carbs; 4.9g Protein; 3.8g Sugars

Ingredients

- 1/2 cup coconut shreds
- 1 tablespoon sunflower seeds
- 2 tablespoons flax seeds
- 2 cardamom pods, crushed slightly
- 1 teaspoon ground cinnamon
- 1 teaspoon Stevia powdered extract
- 1 teaspoon rosewater
- 1/2 cup water
- 1 cup coconut milk

Directions

1. Add all ingredients to the Instant Pot.
2. Secure the lid. Choose "Manual" mode and High pressure; cook for 5 minutes. Once cooking is complete, use a quick pressure release; carefully remove the lid.
3. Ladle into two serving bowls and serve warm. Enjoy!

Cheesecake Tropicana

Preparation Time: 30 minutes + chilling time

Servings 5

Nutritional Values per serving: 268 Calories; 22.7g Fat; 6.6g Total Carbs; 9.5g Protein; 4.2g Sugars

Ingredients

- 9 ounces cream cheese
- 1/3 cup Swerve
- 1/2 teaspoon ginger powder
- 1 teaspoon grated orange zest
- 1 teaspoon vanilla extract
- 3 eggs
- 4 tablespoons double cream
- 1 tablespoon Swerve
- 1 navel orange, peeled and sliced

Directions

1. Start by adding 1 ½ cups of water and a metal rack to your Instant Pot. Now, spritz a baking pan with a nonstick cooking spray.
2. Beat cream cheese, 1/3 cup of Swerve, ginger, grated orange zest, and vanilla with an electric mixer.
3. Now, gradually fold in the eggs, and continue to mix until everything is well incorporated. Press this

mixture into the prepared baking pan and cover with foil.

4. Secure the lid. Choose "Bean/Chili" mode and High pressure; cook for 25 minutes. Once cooking is complete, use a natural pressure release; carefully remove the lid.

5. Mix the cream and 1 tablespoon of Swerve; spread this topping on the cake. Allow it to cool on a wire rack.

6. Then, transfer your cake to the refrigerator. Garnish with orange slices and serve well chilled. Bon appétit!

Classic Holiday Custard

Preparation Time: 20 minutes + chilling time

Servings 4

Nutritional Values per serving: 201 Calories; 17.7g Fat; 6.2g Total Carbs; 4.2g Protein; 1.2g Sugars

Ingredients

- 5 egg yolks
- 1/3 cup coconut milk, unsweetened
- 1/2 teaspoon vanilla extract
- 1 teaspoon monk fruit powder
- 1 tablespoon butterscotch flavoring
- 1/2 stick butter, melted

Directions

1. Blend the egg yolks with coconut milk, vanilla extract, monk fruit powder, and butterscotch flavoring.
2. Then, stir in the butter; stir until everything is well incorporated. Divide the mixture among four Mason jars and cover them with lids.
3. Add 1 ½ cups of water and a metal rack to the Instant Pot. Now, lower your jars onto the rack.
4. Secure the lid. Choose "Manual" mode and Low pressure; cook for 15 minutes. Once cooking is complete, use a natural pressure release; carefully remove the lid. Serve
5. Place in your refrigerator until ready to serve. Bon appétit!

Blackberry Espresso Brownies

Preparation Time: 30 minutes

Servings 8

Nutritional Values per serving: 151 Calories; 13.6g Fat; 6.7g Total Carbs; 4.1g Protein; 1.1g Sugars

Ingredients

- 4 eggs
- 1 ¼ cups coconut cream
- 1 teaspoon Stevia liquid concentrate
- 1/3 cup cocoa powder, unsweetened
- 1/2 teaspoon grated nutmeg
- 1/2 teaspoon cinnamon powder
- 1 teaspoon espresso coffee
- 1 teaspoon pure almond extract
- 1 teaspoon pure vanilla extract
- 1 teaspoon baking powder
- A pinch of kosher salt
- 1 cup blackberries, fresh or frozen (thawed

Instructions

1. Start by adding 1 ½ cups of water and a metal rack to your Instant Pot. Now, spritz a baking pan with a nonstick cooking spray.

2. Now, mix eggs, coconut cream, Stevia, cocoa powder, nutmeg, cinnamon, coffee, pure almond extract vanilla, baking powder, and salt with an electric mixer.
3. Crush the blackberries with a fork. After that, fold in your blackberries into the prepared mixture.
4. Pour the batter into the prepared pan.
5. Secure the lid. Choose "Bean/Chili" mode and High pressure; cook for 25 minutes. Once cooking is complete, use a natural pressure release; carefully remove the lid. Bon appétit!

Sweet Porridge with Blueberries

Preparation Time: 10 minutes

Servings 4

Nutritional Values per serving: 219 Calories; 18.2g Fat; 6.2g Total Carbs; 5.6g Protein; 2.9g Sugars

Ingredients

- 6 tablespoons golden flax meal
- 6 tablespoons coconut flour
- 2 cups water
- 1/4 teaspoon freshly grated nutmeg
- 1/4 teaspoon Himalayan salt
- 3 egg, whisked
- 1/2 stick butter, softened
- 4 tablespoons double cream
- 4 tablespoons monk fruit powder
- 1 cup blueberries

Directions

1. Add all ingredients to the Instant Pot.
2. Secure the lid. Choose "Manual" mode and High pressure; cook for 5 minutes. Once cooking is complete, use a quick pressure release; carefully remove the lid.
3. Serve garnished with some extra berries if desired. Enjoy!

Vanilla Berry Cupcakes

Preparation Time: 35 minutes

Servings 6

Nutritional Values per serving: 403 Calories; 42.1g Fat; 4.1g Total Carbs; 4.2g Protein; 2.1g Sugars

Ingredients

- Cupcakes:
- 1/2 cup coconut flour
- 1/2 cup almond flour
- 1/2 teaspoon baking soda
- 1 teaspoon baking powder
- A pinch of salt
- A pinch of grated nutmeg
- 1 teaspoon ginger powder
- 1 stick butter, at room temperature
- 1/2 cup Swerve
- 3 eggs, beaten
- 1/2 teaspoon pure coconut extract
- 1/2 teaspoon pure vanilla extract
- 1/2 cup double cream
- Frosting:
- 1 stick butter, at room temperature
- 1/2 cup Swerve

- 1 teaspoon pure vanilla extract
- 1/2 teaspoon coconut extract
- 6 tablespoons coconut, shredded
- 3 tablespoons raspberry, puréed
- 6 frozen raspberries

Directions

1. Start by adding 1 ½ cups of water and a rack to your Instant Pot.
2. In a mixing dish, thoroughly combine the cupcake ingredients. Divide the batter between silicone cupcake liners. Cover with a piece of foil.
3. Place the cupcakes on the rack.
4. Secure the lid. Choose "Manual" mode and High pressure; cook for 25 minutes. Once cooking is complete, use a natural pressure release; carefully remove the lid.
5. In the meantime, thoroughly combine the frosting ingredients. Put this mixture into a piping bag and top your cupcakes.
6. Garnish with frozen raspberries and enjoy!

Mini Cheesecakes with Berries

Preparation Time: 25 minutes

Servings 6

Nutritional Values per serving: 232 Calories; 22.1g Fat; 4.8g Total Carbs; 5.7g Protein; 1.9g Sugars

Ingredients

- 1/4 cup sesame seed flour
- 1/4 cup hazelnut flour
- 1/2 cup coconut flour
- 1 ½ teaspoons baking powder
- A pinch of kosher salt
- A pinch of freshly grated nutmeg
- 1/2 teaspoon ground star anise
- 1/2 teaspoon ground cinnamon
- 1/2 stick butter
- 1 cup Swerve
- 2 eggs, beaten
- 1/2 cup cream cheese
- 1/3 cup fresh mixed berries
- 1/2 vanilla paste

Directions

1. Start by adding 1 ½ cups of water and a rack to your Instant Pot.
2. In a mixing dish, thoroughly combine all of the above ingredients. Divide the batter between lightly greased ramekins. Cover with a piece of foil.
3. Place the ramekins on the rack.
4. Secure the lid. Choose "Manual" mode and High pressure; cook for 20 minutes. Once cooking is complete, use a natural pressure release; carefully remove the lid.

Special Berry Crisp with Cinnamon

Preparation Time: 15 minutes

Servings 4

Nutritional Values per serving: 255 Calories; 24.6g Fat; 5.6g Total Carbs; 3.4g Protein; 2.5g Sugars

Ingredients

- 1/2 pound blackberries
- 1 teaspoon ground cinnamon
- 1/4 teaspoon grated nutmeg
- 1/2 teaspoon ground cardamom
- 1/2 teaspoon vanilla paste
- 1/2 cup water
- 1/4 cup Swerve
- 5 tablespoons coconut oil, melted
- 1/2 cup almonds, roughly chopped
- 1/4 cup coconut flour
- 1/4 teaspoon Stevia
- A pinch of salt

Directions

1. Place blackberries on the bottom of your Instant Pot. Sprinkle with cinnamon, nutmeg, and cardamom. Add vanilla, water and Swerve.
2. In a mixing bowl, thoroughly combine the remaining ingredients. Drop by the spoonful on top of the blackberries.
3. Secure the lid. Choose "Manual" mode and High pressure; cook for 10 minutes. Once cooking is complete, use a natural pressure release; carefully remove the lid.
4. Serve at room temperature and enjoy!

Yummy Fire Cheesecake

Preparation Time: 40 minutes

Servings 6

Nutritional Values per serving: 373 Calories; 36.7g Fat; 5.1g Total Carbs; 8g Protein; 2.6g Sugars

Ingredients

- 1/2 cup almond flour
- 1/2 cup coconut flour
- 4 tablespoons coconut oil, melted
- 3/4 pound cream cheese, at room temperature
- 3/4 cup Swerve
- 3 eggs
- A pinch of salt
- A pinch of grated nutmeg
- 1/2 teaspoon ground cinnamon
- 1/2 teaspoon ground star anise
- 1 teaspoon vanilla extract
- 1 teaspoon red food coloring

Directions

1. Start by adding 1 ½ cups of water and a metal rack to your Instant Pot.

2. In a mixing bowl, thoroughly combine almond flour, coconut flour, and coconut oil. Press this mixture into a lightly greased cheesecake pan.
3. In another mixing bowl, beat the cream cheese together with Swerve. Fold in the eggs, one at a time, and continue to beat until well mixed.
4. Then, add the spices and extract; mix until everything is well incorporated. Spread the filling over the top of your cheesecake. Lower the pan onto the rack.
5. Secure the lid. Choose "Bean/Chili" mode and High pressure; cook for 35 minutes. Once cooking is complete, use a natural pressure release; carefully remove the lid. Bon appétit!

Classic Carrot Cake

Preparation Time: 35 minutes

Servings 8

Nutritional Values per serving: 381 Calories; 35.1g Fat; 4.4g Total Carbs; 10.3g Protein; 1.7g Sugars

Ingredients

- Carrot Cake:
- 2 cups carrots, grated
- 1 cup almond flour
- 1/2 cup coconut, shredded
- 1/4 cup hazelnuts, chopped
- 1/4 teaspoon ground cloves
- 1/4 teaspoon grated nutmeg
- 1/2 teaspoon ground cinnamon
- 1/2 teaspoon baking soda
- 1 teaspoon baking powder
- 4 tablespoons Swerve
- 1 teaspoon pure vanilla extract
- 4 eggs, beaten
- 1 stick butter, melted
- Cream Cheese Frosting:

1 cup cream cheese

2 tablespoons Swerve

1/2 teaspoon pure vanilla extract

Directions

1. Start by adding 1 ½ cups of water and a metal rack to your Instant Pot. Now, spritz a cheesecake pan with a nonstick cooking spray.
2. In a mixing bowl, thoroughly combine dry ingredients for the cake. Then, mix the wet ingredients until everything is well combined.
3. Pour the wet mixture into the dry mixture and stir to combine well. Spoon the batter into the cheesecake pan.
4. Cover with a sheet of foil. Lower the pan onto the rack.
5. Secure the lid. Choose "Bean/Chili" mode and High pressure; cook for 30 minutes. Once cooking is complete, use a quick pressure release; carefully remove the lid.
6. Meanwhile, mix the frosting ingredients. Frost the carrot cake and serve chilled. Enjoy!

Classic Brownie with Blackberry-Goat Cheese Swirl

Preparation Time: 30 minutes

Servings 8

Nutritional Values per serving: 309 Calories; 27.6g Fat; 3.4g Total Carbs; 10.8g Protein; 1.1g Sugars

Ingredients

- Brownies:
- 5 tablespoons coconut oil, melted
- 1 cup Swerve
- 1/4 cup cocoa powder, unsweetened
- 3 teaspoons water
- 1/2 teaspoon vanilla extract
- 3 eggs, beaten
- 1/4 cup golden flax meal
- 3/4 cup almond flour
- 1/2 teaspoon baking soda
- 1/2 teaspoon baking powder
- A pinch of salt
- A pinch of grated nutmeg
- 1/4 cup chocolate chunks, sugar-free

Blackberry Goat Cheese Swirl:

- 2 tablespoons unsalted butter, softened
- 4 ounces goat cheese, softened
- 2 ounces cream cheese, softened
- 1 cup blackberries, fresh or frozen (thawed
- 1 tablespoon Swerve
- 1/2 teaspoon almond extract
- A pinch of salt

Directions

1. Start by adding 1 ½ cups of water and a metal rack to your Instant Pot. Now, spritz a square cake pan with a nonstick cooking spray.
2. Mix the coconut oil with Swerve, cocoa powder, water, and vanilla until well combined. Mix in the eggs, flour, baking soda, baking powder, salt, and nutmeg.
3. Mix until smooth and creamy. Add the chocolate and mix one more time. Add the batter to the prepared pan.
4. Secure the lid. Choose "Manual" mode and High pressure; cook for 25 minutes. Once cooking is complete, use a quick pressure release; carefully remove the lid.
5. Invert your brownie onto a platter. Allow it to cool to room temperature.

6. Meanwhile, make the blackberry-goat cheese swirl. Beat the butter and cheese with an electric mixer; add blackberries, Swerve, almond extract and salt and continue to beat until light and fluffy.
7. Drop this mixture on top of your brownie in spoonfuls; then swirl it with a knife. Bon appétit!

Special Birthday Cake

Preparation Time: 35 minutes + chilling time

Servings 8

Nutritional Values per serving: 230 Calories; 18.8g Fat; 6.1g Total Carbs; 8.9g Protein; 1.4g Sugars

Ingredients

- Batter:
- 1 cup hazelnut flour
- 2 tablespoons arrowroot starch
- 1/2 cup cocoa powder
- 1 ¼ teaspoons baking powder
- 1/4 teaspoon kosher salt
- 1/4 teaspoon freshly grated nutmeg
- 6 eggs, whisked
- 8 tablespoons coconut oil, melted
- 1 teaspoon pure vanilla extract
- 1/2 teaspoon pure hazelnut extract
- 2/3 cup Swerve
- 1/3 cup full-fat milk
- Hazelnut Ganache:
- 1/2 cup heavy cream
- 5 ounces dark chocolate, sugar-free
- 2 tablespoons coconut oil

Directions

1. Start by adding 1 ½ cups of water and a metal rack to your Instant Pot. Now, lightly grease a baking pan with a nonstick cooking spray.
2. In a mixing bowl, thoroughly combine dry ingredients for the batter. In another bowl, mix wet ingredients for the batter.
3. Add wet mixture to the dry mixture; mix to combine well. Pour the mixture into the prepared baking pan.
4. Secure the lid. Choose "Bean/Chili" mode and High pressure; cook for 30 minutes. Once cooking is complete, use a natural pressure release; carefully remove the lid.
5. Now, place the cake pan on a wire rack until it is cool to the touch. Allow it to cool completely before frosting.
6. Meanwhile, make your ganache. In a medium pan, bring the heavy cream to a boil. Turn the heat off as soon as you see the bubbles.
7. Add chocolate and coconut oil and whisk to combine well. Frost the cake and serve well chilled.

Holiday Blueberry Pudding

Preparation Time: 20 minutes

Servings 6

Nutritional Values per serving: 240 Calories; 20.5g Fat; 5.4g Total Carbs; 4.8g Protein; 3.1g Sugars

Ingredients

- 1 cup almond flour
- 3 tablespoons sunflower seed flour
- 1/2 cup Swerve
- 1/2 teaspoon baking soda
- 1 teaspoon baking powder
- 1/4 cup coconut cream
- 1/4 cup water
- 1/4 cup coconut oil, softened
- 2 tablespoons dark rum
- 1/2 teaspoon vanilla
- 1/2 cup blueberries

Directions

1. Start by adding 1 ½ cups of water and a metal trivet to your Instant Pot.
2. Mix all ingredients, except blueberries, until everything is well incorporated. Spoon the mixture into a lightly greased baking pan.

3. Fold in blueberries and gently stir to combine. Lower the baking dish onto the trivet.
4. Secure the lid. Choose "Bean/Chili" mode and High pressure; cook for 15 minutes. Once cooking is complete, use a natural pressure release; carefully remove the lid.
5. Allow the cobbler to cool slightly before serving. Bon appétit!

Fluffy Strawberry Cake

Preparation Time: 35 MIN

Serving: 6

Ingredients:

- 2 cups almond flour
- 1 cup coconut flour
- ¼ cup unsweetened cocoa powder
- 1 tsp baking soda
- ½ tsp baking powder
- ½ tsp salt
- 1 cup unsweetened almond milk
- 3 eggs
- 2 egg whites
- 3 cups whipped cream, sugar-free
- 1 tsp stevia extract
- 2 tsp strawberry extract

Directions:

1. Line a 7-inches springform pan with some parchment paper. Set aside.
2. In a large mixing bowl, combine almond flour, coconut flour, cocoa powder, baking soda, baking powder, and salt. Mix well and gradually add milk. With a paddle attachment on, beat well on high speed. Now add eggs,

one at the time, beating constantly. Finally, add egg whites and mix until completely incorporated. Transfer the mixture to the prepared springform pan and flatten the surface with a kitchen spatula. Cover loosely with some aluminum foil.

3. Plug in your Instant Pot and pour in 1 cup of water. Set the trivet in the stainless steel insert and gently place the springform on top.
4. Seal the lid and set the steam release handle to the 'Sealing' position. Press the 'Manual' button and set the timer for 20 minutes.
5. When done, move the steam valve to the 'Venting' position to release the pressure.
6. Open the lid and carefully remove the springform pan. Place on a wire rack and cool to a room temperature.
7. Meanwhile, place whipped cream, stevia, and strawberry extract in a large bowl. Using a hand mixer, beat well until fully combined.
8. Pour the mixture over the chilled crust and refrigerate for one hour before use.

Nutritional Values per serving:

Calories 195

Total Fats 16.4g

Net Carbs: 4.2g

Protein 5.7g

Fiber: 3.8g

Chocolate Cheesecake

Preparation Time: 45 MIN

Serving: 10

Ingredients:

- 1 cup almond flour
- 1 cup coconut flour
- 1 cup unsweetened cocoa powder, divided in half
- ¼ cup swerve
- ½ cup butter
- 2 large eggs
- 4 cups cream cheese
- ¾ cup heavy cream
- 1 tsp vanilla extract
- ½ tsp stevia powder
- 2 tbsp. oil

Directions:

1. In a large bowl, combine together almond flour, coconut flour, unsweetened cocoa powder, and swerve. Mix well and transfer to a food processor along with butter and eggs. Process well and set aside.
2. Brush a 7-inches springform pan with oil and line with some parchment paper. Add the crust mixture and press well with your hands.

3. Plug in your instant pot and pour into 1 ½ cups of water. Place the trivet in the stainless steel insert and gently put the springform on top. Cover with some aluminum foil to prevent condensate dripping.
4. Seal the lid and set the steam release handle to 'Sealing' position. Press the 'Manual' button and set the timer for 15 minutes.
5. When you hear the cooker's end signal, release the pressure naturally for 10-12 minutes. Move the pressure valve to the 'Venting' position to release any remaining pressure.
6. Open the lid and gently remove the springform pan. Chill to a room temperature.
7. Place cream cheese, heavy cream, vanilla extract, and stevia powder in a blender. Pulse to combine and pour the mixture over the chilled crust.
8. Refrigerate overnight.

Nutritional Values per serving:

Calories 548

Total Fats 52g

Net Carbs: 7.4g

Protein 12g

Fiber: 6.8g

Raspberry Compote

Preparation Time: 45 MIN

Serving: 4

Ingredients:

- 2 cups raspberries
- 1 cup swerve
- 1 tsp freshly grated lemon zest
- 1 tsp vanilla extract

Directions:

1. Plug in your instant pot and press the 'Saute' button. Add raspberries, swerve, lemon zest, and vanilla extract. Stir well and pour in 1 cup of water. Cook for 5 minutes, stirring constantly.
2. Now pour in 2 more cups of water and press the 'Cancel' button. Seal the lid and set the steam release handle to the 'Sealing' position. Press the 'Manual' button and set the timer for 15 minutes on low pressure.
3. When you hear the cooker's end signal, press the 'Cancel' button and release the pressure naturally for 10-15 minutes. Move the pressure handle to the 'Venting' position to release any remaining pressure and open the lid.

4. Optionally, stir some more lemon juice and transfer to serving bowls.
5. Chill to a room temperature and refrigerate for one hour before serving.

Nutritional Values per serving:

Calories 48

Total Fats 0.5g

Net Carbs: 5g

Protein 1g

Fiber: 5.3g

Chocolate Cream

Preparation Time: 25 MIN

Serving: 4

Ingredients:

- 2 heavy cream
- ¼ cup unsweetened dark chocolate, chopped
- 3 eggs
- 1 tsp orange zest
- 1 tsp stevia powder
- 1 tsp vanilla extract
- ½ tsp salt

Directions:

1. Plug in your instant pot and press the 'Saute' button. Add heavy cream, chopped chocolate, stevia powder, vanilla extract, orange zest, and salt. Stir well and simmer until the chocolate has completely melted. Press the 'Cancel' button and crack eggs, one at the time, stirring constantly. Remove from the instant pot.
2. Transfer the mixture to 4 mason jars with loose lids.
3. Pour 2 cups of water in your instant pot and set the trivet in the stainless steel insert. Add jars and seal the lid.

4. Set the steam release handle and press the 'Manual' button. Set the timer for 10 minutes.
5. When done, perform a quick release by moving the steam valve to the 'Venting' position.
6. Open the lid and remove the jars. Chill to a room temperature and then transfer to the refrigerator.
7. Top with some whipped cream before serving.

Nutritional Values per serving:

Calories 267

Total Fats 26.2g

Net Carbs: 2.4g

Protein 5.6g

Fiber: 0.2g

Butter Pancakes

Preparation Time: 15 MIN

Serving: 6

Ingredients:

- 2 cups cream cheese
- 2 cups almond flour
- 6 large eggs
- ¼ tsp salt
- 2 tbsp. butter
- ¼ tsp ground ginger
- ½ tsp cinnamon powder

Directions:

1. In a large mixing bowl, combine cream cheese, eggs, and one tablespoon of butter. With a paddle attachment on, beat well on high speed until light and creamy. Slowly add flour beating constantly. Finally, add salt, ginger, and cinnamon. Continue to beat until fully incorporated.
2. Plug in your instant pot and press the 'Saute' button. Grease the stainless steel insert with the remaining butter and heat up.

3. Pour in about ½ cup of the batter and cook for 2-3 minutes or until golden color. Repeat the process with the remaining batter.
4. Serve warm.

Nutritional Values per serving:

Calories 432

Total Fats 40.2g

Net Carbs: 3.5g

Protein 14.2g

Fiber: 1g

Lemon Cupcakes with Blueberries

Preparation Time: 35 MIN

Serving: 6

Ingredients:

- 2 cups almond flour
- 2/3 tsp baking powder
- ¼ tsp baking soda
- ½ tsp xanthan gum
- 1 cup swerve
- 3 eggs
- 1 cup almond milk, unsweetened
- ¼ cup blueberries
- 1 tbsp. butter, softened
- 1 tbsp. coconut oil
- 1 tbsp. lemon zest, freshly grated
- 1 tsp vanilla extract

Directions:

1. Combine all dry ingredients in a large mixing bowl. Mix well and gradually add milk. Beat well on medium speed adding eggs, one at the time. Add butter, coconut oil, lemon zest, and vanilla extract. Mix until fully incorporated. Fold in blueberries and transfer to 12-cup silicone cupcake pan.

2. Plug in your instant pot and pour in 1 cup of water. Set the trivet in the stainless steel insert and place the silicone pan on top. Cover loosely with some aluminum foil and seal the lid.
3. Set the steam release handle to the 'Sealing' position and press the 'Manual' button. Set the timer for 25 minutes.
4. When done, perform a quick pressure release and open the lid. Gently remove the muffin pan from your instant pot and cool completely before serving.

Nutritional Values per serving:

Calories 223

Total Fats 20.4g

Net Carbs: 3.8g

Protein 5.9g

Fiber: 2.9g

Chocolate Brownies

Preparation Time: 30 MIN

Serving: 8

Ingredients:

- ½ cup cocoa powder, unsweetened
- ¼ cup unsweetened dark chocolate chunks
- 1 cup cream cheese
- 2 large eggs
- 3 tbsp. coconut oil
- ½ tsp salt
- ¾ cup swerve

Directions:

1. Combine cream cheese, eggs, and coconut oil in a large mixing bowl. With a paddle attachment on, beat well on medium speed until smooth. Add cocoa powder, salt, swerve, and dark chocolate chunks. Continue to beat for 2 minutes, or until fully incorporated.
2. Brush a 7-inches cake pan with some oil and line with some parchment paper. Dust the paper with some cocoa powder and pour in the batter. Flatten the surface with a kitchen spatula and loosely cover with aluminum foil.

3. Plug in your instant pot and pour in 1 cup of water. Set the steam rack at the bottom of the steel insert and place the cake pan on top.
4. Seal the lid and set the steam release to the 'Sealing' position. Select the 'Manual' mode and set the timer for 20 minutes.
5. When you hear the cooker's end signal, release the pressure naturally for 15 minutes. Open the lid and carefully remove the pan.
6. Cool completely and cut into 8 brownies.

Nutritional Values per serving:

Calories 180

Total Fats 17.5g

Net Carbs: 2.4g

Protein 4.8g

Fiber: 1.7g

Peach Pie

Preparation Time: 40 MIN

Serving: 6

Ingredients:

- 2 cups almond flour
- 1 medium-sized peach, sliced
- ¼ cup raspberries
- 4 large eggs
- 6 tbsp. butter
- 2 tsp baking powder
- ½ tsp salt
- ¼ cup swerve
- ¼ tsp vanilla extract
- 2 tsp lemon zest

Directions:

1. Brush a 7-inches cake pan with oil and line with some parchment paper. Set aside.
2. In a medium-sized bowl, whisk together eggs and swerve. Set aside.
3. In another bowl, combine all the remaining dry ingredients and mix well. Slowly pour in the egg mixture, mixing constantly, and add the remaining

ingredients. Transfer to a mixing bowl and beat for 2 minutes on medium speed.
4. Pour the mixture into the prepared cake pan and shake a couple of times to flatten the surface. Wrap with some aluminum foil.
5. Plug in your instant pot and pour in 1 cup of water. Set the trivet at the bottom of the stainless steel insert and place the wrapped pan on top. Seal the lid and set the steam release handle to the 'Sealing' position.
6. Select the 'Manual' mode and set the timer for 25 minutes.
7. When done, perform a quick release by moving the pressure valve to the 'Venting' position.
8. Open the lid and remove the pan. Cool completely before serving.

Nutritional Values per serving:

Calories 221

Total Fats 19.4g

Net Carbs: 4.4g

Protein 6.6g

Fiber: 1.8g

Almond Butter Cookies

Preparation Time: 40 MIN

Serving: 15

Ingredients:

- 1 ½ cup almond flour
- ½ cup coconut flour
- 3 eggs
- ¾ cup coconut oil, melted
- 3 tbsp. almond butter
- ¼ cup cocoa powder, unsweetened
- ½ cup swerve
- ½ tsp salt

Directions:

1. Plug in your instant pot and pour in 1 cup of water. Set the trivet at the bottom of the stainless steel insert and set aside.
2. Line a round baking pan with some parchment paper and set aside.
3. In a large mixing bowl, combine together almond flour, coconut flour, cocoa butter, swerve, and salt. Add eggs, coconut oil, and almond butter. With a paddle attachment on, beat well on high speed until fully incorporated.

4. Scoop out 15 cookies and place them in the prepared baking pan. You will probably have to do this in several batches. Gently flatten each cookie with the palm of your hand and place the pan in your instant pot. Cover with aluminum foil.
5. Seal the lid and set the steam release handle. Press the 'Manual' button and set the timer for 25 minutes.
6. When done, release the pressure naturally for 15 minutes. Move the pressure handle to the 'Venting' position to release any remaining pressure.
7. Open the lid and remove the pan. Cool to a room temperature and then transfer the cookies to a wire rack to cool completely.

Nutritional Values per serving:

Calories 154

Total Fats 15.3g

Net Carbs: 1.5g

Protein 2.9g

Fiber: 1.9g

Mini Brownie Cakes

Preparation Time: 25 MIN

Serving: 4

Ingredients:

- 1 cup almond flour
- ½ cup cocoa powder, unsweetened
- ¼ cup swerve
- 4 eggs
- ¼ cup unsweetened dark chocolate, cut into chunks
- 1 tsp rum extract
- ½ cup coconut oil

Directions:

1. Plug in your instant pot and pour in 1 cup of water. Set the trivet at the bottom of the stainless steel insert and set aside.
2. In a large mixing bowl, combine together eggs, swerve, dark chocolate chunks, rum extract, and coconut oil. Mix well until light and creamy mixture. Sift almond flour and cocoa powder over the egg mixture and mix well again.
3. Divide the mixture between 4 ramekins and tightly wrap with aluminum foil. Place each ramekin on the trivet and seal the lid.

4. Set the steam release handle to the 'Sealing' position. Press the 'Manual' button and set the timer for 15 minutes.
5. When done, release the pressure naturally for another 15 minutes.
6. Open the lid and gently remove the ramekins using oven mitts. Place on a wire rack and cool completely before serving.

Nutritional Values per serving:

Calories 404

Total Fats 39.1g

Net Carbs: 4.8g

Protein 9.7g

Fiber: 4.7g

Egg Salad

Preparation Time: 30 minutes

Servings 4

Nutritional Values per serving: 342 Calories; 29.2g Fat; 3.2g Total Carbs; 12.7g Protein; 1.6g Sugars

Ingredients

- 6 eggs
- 1/2 pound green beans, trimmed
- 1 cup of water
- 3 slices prosciutto, chopped
- 1/2 cup green onions, chopped
- 1 carrot, shredded
- 1/2 cup mayonnaise
- 1 tablespoon apple cider vinegar
- 1 teaspoon yellow mustard
- 4 tablespoons Gorgonzola cheese, crumbled

Directions

1. Pour the water into the Instant Pot; add a steamer basket to the bottom. Arrange the eggs in a steamer basket.
2. Secure the lid. Choose "Manual" mode and High pressure; cook for 5 minutes. Once cooking is complete, use a natural pressure release; carefully remove the lid.

3. Allow the eggs to cool for 15 minutes. Peel the eggs and cut them into slices.
4. Then, add green beans and 1 cup of water to your Instant Pot.
5. Secure the lid. Choose "Manual" mode and Low pressure; cook for 5 minutes. Once cooking is complete, use a quick pressure release; carefully remove the lid.
6. Transfer green beans to a salad bowl. Add prosciutto, green onions, carrot, mayonnaise, vinegar, and mustard. Top with Gorgonzola cheese and sliced eggs. Enjoy!

Granny's Cheesy Soup

Preparation Time: 25 minutes

Servings 4

Nutritional Values per serving: 530 Calories; 37.6g Fat; 4.2g Total Carbs; 43.1g Protein; 1.9g Sugars

Ingredients

- 2 tablespoons butter, melted
- 1/2 cup leeks, chopped
- 2 chicken breasts, trimmed and cut into bite-sized chunks
- 1 carrot, chopped
- 1 celery stalk, chopped
- 1/2 teaspoon granulated garlic
- 1 teaspoon basil
- 1/2 teaspoon oregano
- 1/2 teaspoon dill weed
- 4 ½ cups vegetable stock
- 3 ounces heavy cream
- 3/4 cup Cheddar cheese, shredded
- 1 heaping tablespoon fresh parsley, roughly chopped

Directions

1. Press the "Sauté" button to heat up your Instant Pot. Now, melt the butter and cook the leeks until tender and fragrant.
2. Add the chicken, carrot, celery, garlic, basil, oregano, dill, and stock.
3. Secure the lid. Choose "Manual" mode and High pressure; cook for 17 minutes. Once cooking is complete, use a natural pressure release; carefully remove the lid.
4. Add cream and cheese, stir, and press the "Sauté" button one more time. Now, cook the soup for a couple of minutes longer or until thoroughly heated.
5. Serve in individual bowls, garnished with fresh parsley. Bon appétit!

Cheesy Spicy Eggs

Preparation Time: 25 minutes

Servings 4

Nutritional Values per serving: 264 Calories; 21.1g Fat; 6g Total Carbs; 11.7g Protein; 3.8g Sugars

Ingredients

- 6 eggs
- 1 teaspoon canola oil
- 1 onion, chopped
- 2 bell peppers, drained and chopped
- Seasoned salt and freshly ground black pepper, to taste
- 1/4 cup mayonnaise
- 1 teaspoon mustard
- 1 tablespoon fresh lemon juice
- 4 tablespoons Colby cheese, grated
- 1 teaspoon smoked Hungarian paprika

Directions

1. Pour the water into the Instant Pot; add a steamer basket to the bottom.
2. Arrange the eggs in a steamer basket if you have one.
3. Secure the lid. Choose "Manual" mode and High pressure; cook for 5 minutes. Once cooking is complete, use a natural pressure release; carefully remove the lid.

4. Allow the eggs to cool for 15 minutes. Peel the eggs and separate egg whites from yolks.
5. Press the "Sauté" button to heat up your Instant Pot; heat the oil. Now, sauté the onion along with peppers until softened. Season with salt and pepper.
6. Add the reserved egg yolks to the pepper mixture. Stir in mayo, mustard, and lemon juice. Now, stuff the egg whites with this mixture.
7. Top with grated Colby cheese and arrange the stuffed eggs on a serving platter. Afterwards, sprinkle Hungarian paprika over eggs and serve.

Savory Egg Custard

Preparation Time: 15 minutes

Servings 3

Nutritional Values per serving: 234 Calories; 16.8g Fat; 3.6g Total Carbs; 16.4g Protein; 1.8g Sugars

Ingredients

- 3 eggs, well beaten
- 1 cup broth, preferably homemade
- Kosher salt and white pepper, to taste
- 1 tablespoon tamari sauce
- 1/2 tablespoon oyster sauce

- 1/2 cup Comté cheese, grated

Directions

1. Place the beaten eggs in a mixing bowl. Slowly and gradually, add broth, whisking constantly as you go.
2. Season with salt and paper. Then, pour this mixture through a strainer. Add tamari sauce and oyster sauce.
3. Pour the mixture into three ramekins. Now, cover the ramekins with a piece of foil. Place the ramekins on the metal trivet.
4. Secure the lid. Choose "Manual" mode and Low pressure; cook for 7 minutes. Once cooking is complete, use a natural pressure release; carefully remove the lid.
5. Top with cheese and serve immediately. Bon appétit!

Indian Style Egg Muffins

Preparation Time: 10 minutes

Servings 5

Nutritional Values per serving: 202 Calories; 13.7g Fat; 4.7g Total Carbs; 15.4g Protein; 2.6g Sugars

Ingredients

- 5 eggs
- Seasoned salt and ground black pepper, to taste
- 2 green chilies, minced
- 5 tablespoons feta cheese, crumbled
- 1/2 tablespoon Chaat masala powder
- 1 tablespoon fresh cilantro, finely chopped

Directions

1. Begin by adding 1 cup of water and a steamer basket to your Instant Pot.
2. Mix all ingredients together; then, spoon the egg/cheese mixture into silicone muffin cups.
3. Next, lower your muffin cups onto the steamer basket.
4. Secure the lid. Choose "Manual" mode and High pressure; cook for 7 minutes. Once cooking is complete, use a quick pressure release; carefully remove the lid.
5. Let your muffins sit for a few minutes before removing from the cups; serve warm. Bon appétit!

Bell Pepper and Egg "Sandwich"

Preparation Time: 10 minutes

Servings 2

Nutritional Values per serving: 320 Calories; 25.5g Fat; 5.1g Total Carbs; 15.7g Protein; 3.3g Sugars

Ingredients

- 2 teaspoons butter
- 5 eggs
- 4 tablespoons whipped cream
- Seasoned salt to taste
- 1/3 teaspoon red pepper flakes, crushed
- 2 bell peppers
- 1/2 tomato, sliced
- 1/2 cucumber, sliced

Directions

1. Press the "Sauté" button to heat up your Instant Pot. Now, warm the butter.
2. Thoroughly combine the eggs, cream, salt, and red pepper. Stir with a wooden spoon until the eggs are softly set.
3. Now, cut the top and bottom off of each pepper; remove seeds and veins. Then, slices each bell pepper in half.
4. Place the scrambled eggs, tomato, and cucumber between the two pieces. Serve and enjoy!

Cheese, Sausage and Vegetable Bake

Preparation Time: 25 minutes

Servings 4

Nutritional Values per serving: 344 Calories; 27.4g Fat; 3g Total Carbs; 20.3g Protein; 1.3g Sugars

Ingredients

- 8 slices pork sausage, chopped
- 1 ½ cups mushrooms, sliced
- 1 garlic clove, minced
- 1 cup kale leaves, torn into pieces
- 7 eggs
- 1/3 cup milk
- 1 cup Manchego cheese, shredded
- Sea salt and freshly ground black pepper, to taste

Directions

1. Press the "Sauté" button to heat up the Instant Pot. Now, cook the sausage until no longer pink.
2. Then, add mushrooms and garlic; continue to cook until they are fragrant; turn off the Instant Pot; add kale and let it sit for 5 minutes.
3. Wipe down your Instant Pot with a damp cloth. Add 1 cup of water and a metal rack. Spritz a baking dish that fits into your Instant Pot.

4. In a mixing bowl, thoroughly combine the eggs, milk, cheese, salt and black pepper; add the sausage/vegetable mixture to the mixing bowl.
5. Spoon the mixture into the baking dish. Lower the baking dish onto the rack.
6. Secure the lid. Choose "Manual" mode and High pressure; cook for 15 minutes. Once cooking is complete, use a quick pressure release; carefully remove the lid. Enjoy!

Avocado, Goat Cheese and Egg Muffins

Preparation Time: 15 minutes

Servings 6

Nutritional Values per serving: 227 Calories; 17.5g Fat; 4.3g Total Carbs; 13.6g Protein; 1.3g Sugars

Ingredients

- 6 whole eggs
- Seasoned salt and freshly ground black pepper
- 1/2 teaspoon cayenne pepper
- 1/2 teaspoon dried dill weed
- 2 tablespoons fresh parsley, chopped
- 1 large-sized avocado, peeled, pitted and chopped
- 1/2 cup tomatoes, chopped
- 5 ounces goat cheese, crumbled

Directions

1. Begin by adding 1 cup of water and a steamer basket to your Instant Pot.
2. Mix all ingredients together; then, spoon the mixture into silicone muffin cups.
3. Next, lower your muffin cups onto the steamer basket.
4. Secure the lid. Choose "Manual" mode and High pressure; cook for 7 minutes. Once cooking is complete, use a quick pressure release; carefully remove the lid.
5. Allow these muffins to rest for 5 to 7 minutes before removing from the cups; serve warm. Bon appétit!

Avocado Boats - Spicy and Stuffed

Preparation Time: 10 minutes

Servings 2

Nutritional Values per serving: 281 Calories; 23.6g Fat; 6g Total Carbs; 10.1g Protein; 0.8g Sugars

Ingredients

- 2 avocados, pitted and cut into halves
- 4 eggs
- Salt and pepper, to taste
- 4 tablespoons Cheddar cheese, freshly grated
- 1 teaspoon Sriracha sauce

Directions

1. Start by adding 1 cup of water and a steamer basket to your Instant Pot.
2. Line the steamer basket with a piece of aluminum foil.
3. Now, spoon out some of the avocado flesh and set it aside for another use (for example, you can make guacamole. Arrange avocado halves on your steamer basket.
4. Add an egg to each avocado cavity. Sprinkle with salt and pepper. Top with cheese and drizzle Sriracha sauce over them.
5. Secure the lid. Choose "Manual" mode and High pressure; cook for 3 minutes. Once cooking is complete, use a natural pressure release; carefully remove the lid. Serve warm and enjoy!

Cheesy Beer Dip

Preparation Time: 10 minutes

Servings 10

Nutritional Values per serving: 220 Calories; 14.9g Fat; 2.9g Total Carbs; 18.1g Protein; 1.7g Sugars

Ingredients

- 16 ounces Cottage cheese, softened
- 5 ounces goat cheese, softened
- 1/2 teaspoon garlic powder
- 1 teaspoon stone-ground mustard
- 1/2 cup chicken stock, preferably homemade
- 1/2 cup lager beer
- 6 ounces pancetta, chopped
- 1 cup Monterey-Jack cheese, shredded
- 2 tablespoons fresh chives, roughly chopped

Directions

1. Add Cottage cheese, goat cheese, garlic powder, mustard, chicken stock, beer, and pancetta to the Instant Pot.
2. Secure the lid. Choose "Manual" mode and High pressure; cook for 4 minutes. Once cooking is complete, use a quick pressure release; carefully remove the lid.
3. Press the "Sauté" button to heat up your Instant Pot. Add Monterey-Jack cheese and stir until everything is thoroughly warmed.
4. Sprinkle with fresh chopped chives and serve. Bon appétit!

Healthy Breakfast Wraps

Preparation Time: 10 minutes

Servings 4

Nutritional Values per serving: 202 Calories; 13.7g Fat; 4.7g Total Carbs; 15.4g Protein; 2.6g Sugars

Ingredients

- 4 eggs, whisked
- 1/3 cup double cream
- 2 ounces Mozzarella cheese, crumbled
- 1/3 teaspoon red pepper flakes, crushed
- Salt, to taste
- 8 leaves of Looseleaf lettuce

Directions

1. Begin by adding 1 cup of water and a metal rack to your Instant Pot. Spritz a baking dish with a nonstick cooking spray.
2. Then, thoroughly combine the eggs, double cream, cheese, red pepper, and salt. Spoon this combination into the baking dish.
3. Secure the lid. Choose "Manual" mode and High pressure; cook for 3 minutes. Once cooking is complete, use a natural pressure release; carefully remove the lid.
4. Divide the egg mixture among lettuce leaves, wrap each leaf, and serve immediately. Bon appétit!

Keto Cheesy Pizza

Preparation Time: 20 minutes

Servings 6

Nutritional Values per serving: 334 Calories; 25.1g Fat; 5.9g Total Carbs; 20.5g Protein; 2.8g Sugars

Ingredients

- 1 tablespoon olive oil
- 1 large-sized tomato, chopped
- 6 ounces pepperoni
- 1 yellow onion, chopped
- 2 bell peppers, chopped
- 1 cup mozzarella cheese, sliced
- 1/2 cup provolone cheese, sliced
- 3 eggs, whisked
- 1/2 teaspoon dried basil
- 1/2 teaspoon dried oregano
- 1/2 teaspoon dried rosemary
- 1/2 cup Kalamata olives, pitted and halved

Directions

1. Grease the bottom and sides of your Instant Pot with olive oil. Place 1/2 of chopped tomato on the bottom.
2. Then, layer 3 ounces of pepperoni, 1/2 of yellow onion, 1 bell pepper, 1/2 cup of mozzarella cheese and 1/4 cup of provolone cheese.
3. Continue layering until you run out of ingredients. Pour in the whisked eggs. Afterwards, sprinkle seasonings and olives over the top.
4. Secure the lid. Choose "Manual" mode and High pressure; cook for 15 minutes. Once cooking is complete, use a natural pressure release; carefully remove the lid. Serve warm.

Peppery Habanero Eggs

Preparation Time: 25 minutes

Servings 4

Nutritional Values per serving: 338 Calories; 25.7g Fat; 5.8g Total Carbs; 19.8g Protein; 2.8g Sugars

Ingredients

- 8 eggs
- 2 teaspoons habanero chili pepper, minced
- 1 teaspoon cumin seeds
- 1/4 cup sour cream
- 1/4 cup mayonnaise
- 1 teaspoon stone-ground mustard
- 1/2 teaspoon cayenne pepper
- Sea salt and freshly ground black pepper, to taste

1. **Directions**
2. Pour 1 cup of water into the Instant Pot; add a steamer basket to the bottom.
3. Arrange the eggs in the steamer basket.
4. Secure the lid. Choose "Manual" mode and High pressure; cook for 5 minutes. Once cooking is complete, use a natural pressure release; carefully remove the lid.
5. Allow the eggs to cool for 15 minutes. Peel the eggs and separate egg whites from yolks.

6. Press the "Sauté" button to heat up your Instant Pot; heat the oil. Now, sauté habanero chili pepper and cumin seeds until they are fragrant.
7. Add the reserved egg yolks to the pepper mixture. Stir in sour cream, mayonnaise, mustard, cayenne pepper, salt, and black pepper. Now, stuff the egg whites with this mixture. Bon appétit!

Egg Salad with Mustard Seed Dressing

Preparation Time: 25 minutes

Servings 4

Nutritional Values per serving: 340 Calories; 27.5g Fat; 5.1g Total Carbs; 16.4g Protein; 1.9g Sugars

Ingredients

- 5 medium-sized eggs
- 1/2 pound kale leaves, torn into pieces
- 1/2 cup radishes, sliced
- 1 white onion, thinly sliced
- 2 tablespoons champagne vinegar
- 1/2 tablespoon poppy seeds
- Sea salt and white pepper, to taste
- 1/2 teaspoon cayenne pepper
- 1 teaspoon yellow mustard
- 1/4 cup extra-virgin olive oil
- 3 ounces goat cheese, crumbled

Directions

1. Pour 1 cup of water into the Instant Pot; add a steamer basket to the bottom.
2. Arrange the eggs in the steamer basket.
3. Secure the lid. Choose "Manual" mode and High pressure; cook for 5 minutes. Once cooking is complete, use a natural pressure release; carefully remove the lid.
4. Allow the eggs to cool for 15 minutes. Then, place them in your refrigerator and reserve.
5. Then, place kale in the steamer basket.
6. Secure the lid. Choose "Manual" mode and High pressure; cook for 1 minute. Once cooking is complete, use a quick pressure release; carefully remove the lid.
7. Now, place radishes and onion in a salad bowl. Add kale and sliced eggs.
8. In a mixing dish, thoroughly combine vinegar, poppy seeds, salt, white pepper, cayenne pepper, and olive oil.
9. Pour the dressing over your salad. Top with goat cheese and serve well-chilled. Bon appétit!

Egg Salad Bowl

Preparation Time: 25 minutes

Servings 4

Nutritional Values per serving: 276 Calories; 22.6g Fat; 6.7g Total Carbs; 12.5g Protein; 1.4g Sugars

Ingredients

- 8 eggs
- 1 avocado, pitted, peeled and chopped
- 1/4 mayonnaise
- 1 tablespoon fresh lime juice
- 1 tablespoon champagne vinegar
- 1 teaspoon ground mustard
- Sea salt and ground black pepper, to taste
- 1/2 teaspoon celery seeds
- 8 black olives, pitted and sliced
- 1/2 cup basil leaves, loosely packed

Directions

1. Place 1 cup of water and a steamer basket in your Instant Pot. Now, arrange the eggs on the steamer basket.
2. Secure the lid. Choose "Manual" mode and Low pressure; cook for 5 minutes. Once cooking is complete, use a quick pressure release; carefully remove the lid.

3. Allow the eggs to cool for 15 minutes. Peel the eggs and slice them lengthwise.
4. Place avocado, mayonnaise, lemon juice, vinegar, mustard, salt, black pepper, celery seeds in a serving bowl; stir to combine well.
5. Top with the reserved eggs, olives and basil. Enjoy!

Casserole with Asparagus and Cheese

Preparation Time: 25 minutes

Servings 6

Nutritional Values per serving: 272 Calories; 21.1g Fat; 4.7g Total Carbs; 15.5g Protein; 2.3g Sugars

Ingredients

- 1 tablespoon butter, softened
- 1/2 cup leeks, chopped
- 2 garlic cloves, minced
- 10 asparagus spears, chopped
- 6 eggs, beaten
- 4 tablespoons milk
- 3 tablespoons cream cheese
- Kosher salt and white pepper, to taste
- 1/2 teaspoon thyme, minced
- 1/2 teaspoon rosemary, minced
- 1 cup Colby cheese, shredded

Directions

1. Press the "Sauté" button to heat up the Instant Pot. Now, melt the butter and sauté the leeks until softened.
2. Add garlic and cook an additional 30 seconds. Turn off your Instant Pot. Add the remaining ingredients and mix to combine.
3. Spoon the mixture into lightly greased ramekins.
4. Wipe down your Instant Pot with a damp cloth. Place 1 cup of water and a rack in your Instant Pot.
5. Lower the ramekins onto the rack. Cover them with a piece of foil.
6. Secure the lid. Choose "Soup/Broth" mode and Low pressure; cook for 20 minutes. Once cooking is complete, use a quick pressure release; carefully remove the lid.Bon appétit!

Festive Breakfast Eggs

Preparation Time: 10 minutes

Servings 3

Nutritional Values per serving: 259 Calories; 19.2g Fat; 2g Total Carbs; 17.9g Protein; 1.3g Sugars

Ingredients

- 6 large eggs
- Salt and paprika, to taste

Directions

1. Add 1 cup of water and a metal trivet to the Instant Pot.
2. Spritz six silicone cups with a nonstick cooking spray. Crack an egg into each cup.
3. Then, lower the silicone cups onto the metal trivet.
4. Secure the lid. Choose "Steam" mode and High pressure; cook for 4 minutes. Once cooking is complete, use a quick pressure release; carefully remove the lid.
5. Season your eggs with salt and paprika. Bon appétit!

Green Dip with Cheese and Mustard

Preparation Time: 10 minutes

Servings 8

Nutritional Values per serving: 49 Calories; 3.1g Fat; 1.4g Total Carbs; 3.9g Protein; 0.8g Sugars

Ingredients

- 1 cup mustard greens, chopped
- 4 ounces Cottage cheese, at room temperature
- 1/2 cup goat cheese, at room temperature
- Salt and ground black pepper, to taste
- 1 teaspoon Dijon mustard

Directions

1. Simply throw all of the above ingredients into your Instant Pot.
2. Secure the lid. Choose "Manual" mode and Low pressure; cook for 3 minutes. Once cooking is complete, use a quick pressure release; carefully remove the lid.
3. Serve warm and enjoy!

Cheesy Cauliflower Dip

Preparation Time: 10 minutes

Servings 10

Nutritional Values per serving: 97 Calories; 8.7g Fat; 1.2g Total Carbs; 3.9g Protein; 0.5g Sugars

Ingredients

- 1 cup water
- 1/2 pound cauliflower, broken into florets
- 1/2 cup chicken stock, warm
- 1/2 stick butter
- 1 cup Paneer cheese, crumbled
- 2 tablespoons fresh coriander, chopped
- 1 teaspoon Kala namak
- 1/4 teaspoon black pepper

Directions

1. Start by adding water and a steamer basket to your Instant Pot. Now, place cauliflower florets in the steamer basket.
2. Secure the lid. Choose "Manual" mode and Low pressure; cook for 3 minutes. Once cooking is complete, use a quick pressure release; carefully remove the lid.
3. Then, purée the cauliflower florets in your food processor.
4. Add the remaining ingredients; puree until everything is well combined. Bon appétit!

The Best Keto Breakfast

Preparation Time: 10 minutes

Servings 4

Nutritional Values per serving: 256 Calories; 18.6g Fat; 5.3g Total Carbs; 17g Protein; 2.9g Sugars

Ingredients

- 4 medium-sized Portobello mushrooms, stems removed
- 4 eggs
- 1 red bell pepper, deveined and chopped
- 1 green bell pepper, deveined and chopped
- Sea salt and ground black pepper, to your liking
- 1/2 teaspoon cayenne pepper
- 1/2 teaspoon dried dill weed
- 1 cup Pepper-Jack cheese, grated

Directions

1. Start by adding 1 cup of water and a metal trivet to your Instant Pot. Spritz Portobello mushrooms with a nonstick cooking spray.
2. Mix the eggs, pepper, salt, black pepper, cayenne pepper, and dill; mix until everything is well combined. Spoon this mixture into the prepared mushrooms caps.
3. Place the stuffed mushrooms onto the metal trivet.
4. Secure the lid. Choose "Manual" mode and High pressure; cook for 6 minutes. Once cooking is complete, use a quick pressure release; carefully remove the lid.
5. Top with shredded cheese. Bon appétit!

Yummy Keto Wraps

Preparation Time: 10 minutes

Servings 4

Nutritional Values per serving: 298 Calories; 24.2g Fat; 3.6g Total Carbs; 15.7g Protein; 1.3g Sugars

Ingredients

- 2 teaspoons butter, at room temperature
- 4 eggs
- Salt and red pepper, to taste
- 1/2 cup Cheddar cheese, shredded
- 8 slices mortadella
- 1/4 cup mayonnaise
- 1 tablespoon Dijon mustard
- 8 leaves of Romaine lettuce

Directions

1. Press the "Sauté" button to heat up your Instant Pot. Now, warm the butter.
2. Add the eggs and stir them with a wooden spoon until the eggs are softly set. Add the salt, red pepper, and cheese.
3. Continue to cook an additional 40 seconds or until the cheese is melted. Turn off the Instant Pot.
4. Now, divide the egg/cheese mixture among mortadella slices; add mayo and mustard. Add one leaf of lettuce to each roll.

Sausage and Tomatoes Stew

Preparation time: 10 minutes

Cooking time: 20 minutes

Servings: 4

Ingredients:

- 1 pound pork sausage, sliced
- 14 ounces canned tomatoes, chopped
- 1 yellow onions, chopped
- A pinch of salt and black pepper
- 1 tablespoon avocado oil
- ½ cup beef stock

Directions:

1. Set the instant pot on Sauté mode, add the oil, heat it up, add the onion and the sausage and brown for 5 minutes.
2. Add the rest of the ingredients, put the lid on and cook on Low for 15 minutes.
3. Release the pressure naturally for 10 minutes, divide the stew into bowls and serve.

Nutritional Values per serving: Calories 200, fat 7, fiber 3, carbs 9, protein 12

Rosemary Beef and Parsnips Stew

Preparation time: 10 minutes

Cooking time: 30 minutes

Servings: 4

Ingredients:

- 1 pound beef stew meat, cubed
- 2 tablespoons olive oil
- A pinch of salt and black pepper
- ¼ pound parsnips, sliced
- 4 garlic cloves, minced
- 2 cups beef stock
- 1 tablespoon tomato paste
- A bunch of rosemary, chopped

Directions:

1. Set the instant pot on Sauté mode, add the oil, heat it up, add the beef and the garlic and brown for 5 minutes stirring often.
2. Add the parsnips and the rest of the ingredients, put the lid on and cook on High for 25 minutes.
3. Release the pressure naturally for 10 minutes, divide the stew into bowls and serve.

Nutritional Values per serving: Calories 242, fat 12, fiber 4, carbs 9, protein 13

Italian Chicken and Spinach Stew

Preparation time: 10 minutes

Cooking time: 25 minutes

Servings: 4

Ingredients:

- 1 pound chicken breast, skinless, boneless and cubed
- 1 tablespoon olive oil
- 1 yellow onion, chopped
- 2 cups spinach, torn
- 1 cup chicken stock
- ½ cup tomato sauce
- Salt and black pepper to the taste

Directions:

1. Set your instant pot on Sauté mode, add the oil, heat it up, add the onion and the chicken and brown for 5 minutes.
2. Add the rest of the ingredients, put the lid on and cook on Low for 20 minutes.
3. Release the pressure naturally for 10 minutes, divide the stew into bowls and serve.

Nutritional Values per serving: Calories 263, fat 11, fiber 3, carbs 6, protein 17

Chicken and Okra Stew

Preparation time: 10 minutes

Cooking time: 20 minutes

Servings: 4

Ingredients:

- 1 yellow onion, chopped
- 1 pound chicken breast, skinless, boneless and cubed
- 1 garlic clove, minced
- 2 cups chicken stock
- 14 ounces okra
- 1 teaspoon five spice
- 12 ounces tomato sauce
- A pinch of salt and black pepper
- 2 teaspoons avocado oil
- ½ cup parsley, chopped
- Juice of 1 lime

Directions:

1. Set the instant pot on Sauté mode, add the oil, heat it up, add the meat and the onion and brown for 5 minutes.
2. Add the rest of the ingredients except the parsley, put the lid on and cook on High for 15 minutes.
3. Release the pressure naturally for 10 minutes, add the parsley, divide the stew into bowls and serve.

Nutritional Values per serving: Calories 253, fat 12, fiber 5, carbs 8, protein 16

Peas and Turkey Stew

Preparation time: 10 minutes

Cooking time: 25 minutes

Servings: 4

Ingredients:

- 1 turkey breast, skinless, boneless and cubed
- 4 garlic cloves, minced
- 1 tablespoon olive oil
- 2 celery stalks, chopped
- 1 yellow onion, chopped
- 1 cup peas
- 2 bay leaves
- ¼ teaspoon thyme, dried
- A pinch of salt and black pepper
- 1 and ½ cups chicken stock
- 3 tablespoons tomato paste
- 1 tablespoon cilantro, chopped

Directions:

1. Set your instant pot on sauté mode, add the oil, heat it up, add the meat, garlic and the onion, stir and sauté for 5 minutes.
2. Add the rest of the ingredients except the cilantro, put the lid on and cook on High for 20 minutes.
3. Release the pressure naturally for 10 minutes, discard the bay leaves, add the parsley, divide the stew into bowls and serve.

Nutritional Values per serving: Calories 272, fat 12, fiber 4, carbs 7, protein 11

Turkey and Brussels Sprouts Stew

Preparation time: 10 minutes

Cooking time: 25 minutes

Servings: 4

Ingredients:

- 1 pound turkey breast, skinless, boneless and cubed
- 1 pound Brussels sprouts, halved
- 1 shallot, chopped
- 2 garlic cloves, minced
- 1 tablespoon olive oil
- A pinch of salt and black pepper
- 1 tablespoon thyme, chopped
- ½ tablespoon tarragon, chopped
- 1 tablespoon parsley, chopped
- 1 cup chicken stock
- ½ cup tomato sauce

Directions:

1. Set your instant pot on sauté mode, add the oil, heat it up, add the meat, sprouts, shallot and garlic and brown for 5 minutes.
2. Add the rest of the ingredients, put the lid on and cook on Low for 20 minutes.
3. Release the pressure naturally for 10 minutes, divide the stew into bowls and serve.

Nutritional Values per serving: Calories 239, fat 14, fiber 4, carbs 9, protein 16

Lamb and Peppers Stew

Preparation time: 5 minutes

Cooking time: 20 minutes

Servings: 4

Ingredients:

- 1 pound lamb shoulder, cubed
- 2 tablespoons olive oil
- 1 white onion, chopped
- 2 garlic cloves, minced
- 10 ounces mixed peppers, cut into strips
- 2 cups beef stock
- A pinch of salt and black pepper
- 1 tablespoon basil, dried
- 2 tablespoons thyme, chopped

Directions:

1. Set your instant pot on sauté mode, add the oil, heat it up, add the meat, garlic and onion and sauté for 5 minutes.
2. Add the rest of the ingredients, put the lid on and cook on High for 15 minutes.
3. Release the pressure fast for 5 minutes, divide the stew into bowls and serve.

Nutritional Values per serving: Calories 221, fat 11, fiber 4, carbs 6, protein 14

Cinnamon Pork Stew

Preparation time: 10 minutes

Cooking time: 30 minutes

Servings: 4

Ingredients:

- 1 and ½ pounds pork shoulder, cubed
- 1 yellow onion, chopped
- 2 tablespoons olive oil
- 1 teaspoon cinnamon powder
- 2 garlic cloves, chopped
- A pinch of salt and black pepper
- ½ cup beef stock
- 12 ounces canned tomatoes, chopped
- 1 tablespoon basil, chopped

Directions:

1. Set your instant pot on Sauté mode, add the oil, heat it up, add the meat, onion, garlic and the cinnamon, toss and brown for 5 minutes.
2. Add the rest of the ingredients except the basil, put the lid on and cook on Low for 25 minutes.
3. Release the pressure naturally for 10 minutes, divide the stew into bowls, sprinkle the basil and serve.

Nutritional Values per serving: Calories 231, fat 12, fiber 3, carbs 7, protein 9

Pesto Pork Stew

Preparation time: 10 minutes

Cooking time: 30 minutes

Servings: 4

Ingredients:

- 1 yellow onion, chopped
- 1 pound pork stew meat, cubed
- 1 garlic clove, minced
- 1 cup chicken stock
- 12 ounces tomato sauce
- 1 tablespoon olive oil
- Juice of ½ lemon
- 1 tablespoon parsley, chopped
- 1 tablespoon basil pesto

Directions:

1. Set the instant pot on Sauté mode, add the oil, heat it up, add the meat, onion and garlic and sauté for 5 minutes.
2. Add the rest of the ingredients, put the lid on and cook on Low for 25 minutes.
3. Release the pressure naturally for 10 minutes, divide the stew into bowls and serve.

Nutritional Values per serving: Calories 233, fat 12, fiber 4, carbs 7, protein 15

Beef and Turnips Stew

Preparation time: 10 minutes

Cooking time: 40 minutes

Servings: 6

Ingredients:

- 2 pounds beef stew meat, cubed
- 2 cups chicken stock
- 3 garlic cloves, chopped
- 1 cup tomato sauce
- Salt and black pepper to the taste
- 3 turnips, cut into quarters

Directions:

1. In your instant pot, combine all the ingredients, put the lid on and cook on Low for 40 minutes.
2. Release the pressure naturally for 10 minutes, divide the stew into bowls and serve.

Nutritional Values per serving: Calories 221, fat 12, fiber 4, carbs 7, protein 11

Oregano Lamb and Tomatoes Stew

Preparation time: 10 minutes

Cooking time: 40 minutes

Servings: 4

Ingredients:

- 4 lamb shanks
- 2 tablespoons olive oil
- 1 yellow onion, chopped
- 2 garlic cloves, minced
- 1 and ½ cups tomatoes, cubed
- 1 tablespoon oregano, chopped
- A pinch of salt and black pepper
- 2 cups beef stock

Directions:

1. Set your instant pot on Sauté mode, add the oil, heat it up, add the lamb, and brown for 4 minutes.
2. Add the rest of the ingredients, put the lid on and cook on Low for 35 minutes.
3. Release the pressure naturally for 10 minutes, divide the stew into bowls and serve.

Nutritional Values per serving: Calories 230, fat 14, fiber 4, carbs 7, protein 11

Chili Beef Stew

Preparation time: 5 minutes

Cooking time: 20 minutes

Servings: 4

Ingredients:

- 1 pound beef stew meat, ground
- 2 cups beef stock
- 10 ounces Salsa Verde
- 1 teaspoon chili powder
- A pinch of salt and black pepper
- 1 tablespoon cilantro, chopped

Directions:

1. In your instant pot, combine all the ingredients except the cilantro, put the lid on and cook on High for 20 minutes.
2. Release the pressure fast for 5 minutes, divide the stew into bowls, sprinkle the cilantro on top and serve.

Nutritional Values per serving: Calories 201, fat 7, fiber 4, carbs 7, protein 9

Lemon Kale and Chicken Stew

Preparation time: 10 minutes

Cooking time: 20 minutes

Servings: 4

Ingredients:

- 1 pound chicken breast, skinless, boneless and cubed
- 2 cups kale, torn
- ½ cup chicken stock
- ½ cup tomato sauce
- A pinch of salt and black pepper
- 1 tablespoon cilantro, chopped

Directions:

1. In your instant pot, combine all the ingredients, put the lid on and cook on High for 20 minutes.
2. Release the pressure naturally for 10 minutes, divide the stew into bowls and serve.

Nutritional Values per serving: Calories 192, fat 8, fiber 4, carbs 8, protein 12

Tarragon Beef Stew

Preparation time: 10 minutes

Cooking time: 30 minutes

Servings: 4

Ingredients:

- 1 and ½ pounds beef stew meat, cubed
- 3 garlic cloves, minced
- 2 tablespoons olive oil
- 1 cup tomato sauce
- ½ cup beef stock
- 1 tablespoon tarragon, chopped
- A pinch of salt and black pepper

Directions:

1. Set your instant pot on Sauté mode, add the oil, heat it up, add the meat and the garlic and brown for 5 minutes.
2. Add the rest of the ingredients, put the lid on and cook on Low for 25 minutes.
3. Release the pressure naturally for 10 minutes, divide the stew into bowls and serve.

Nutritional Values per serving: Calories 200, fat 12, fiber 4, carbs 6, protein 9

Bacon and Spinach Stew

Preparation time: 10 minutes

Cooking time: 12 minutes

Servings: 4

Ingredients:

- 2 cups bacon, chopped
- 1 teaspoon olive oil
- 1 pound spinach, torn
- A pinch of salt and black pepper
- ½ cup chicken stock
- 3 tablespoons tomato paste

Directions:

1. Set your instant pot on sauté mode, add the oil, heat it up, add the bacon and cook for 5 minutes.
2. Add the rest of the ingredients, put the lid on and cook on Low for 12 minutes.
3. Release the pressure naturally for 10 minutes, divide the stew into bowls and serve.

Nutritional Values per serving: Calories 195, fat 4, fiber 5, carbs 9, protein 6

Shrimp and Cod Stew

Preparation time: 5 minutes

Cooking time: 12 minutes

Servings: 4

Ingredients:

- 1 pound shrimp, peeled and deveined
- 7 ounces canned tomatoes, chopped
- ½ bunch parsley, chopped
- ¼ cup chicken stock
- 1 pound cod fillets, boneless, skinless and cubed

Directions:

1. In your instant pot, combine all the ingredients, put the lid on and cook on Low for 12 minutes.
2. Release the pressure fast for 5 minutes, divide the mix into bowls and serve.

Nutritional Values per serving: Calories 160, fat 4, fiber 3, carbs 7, protein 9

Green Beans and Chicken Stew

Preparation time: 10 minutes

Cooking time: 15 minutes

Servings: 4

Ingredients:

- 1 tablespoon olive oil
- 2 garlic cloves, minced
- 1 pound chicken breast, skinless, boneless and cubed
- 1 pound green beans, trimmed
- 14 ounces canned tomatoes, chopped
- 1 tablespoon parsley, chopped

Directions:

1. Set the instant pot on Sauté mode, add the oil, heat it up, add the meat and garlic and sauté for 5 minutes.
2. Add the rest of the ingredients, put the lid on and cook on High for 15 minutes.
3. Release the pressure naturally for 10 minutes, divide the stew into bowls and serve.

Nutritional Values per serving: Calories 200, fat 8, fiber 5, carbs 8, protein 10

Turmeric Quinoa and Chicken Stew

Preparation time: 6 minutes

Cooking time: 20 minutes

Servings: 4

Ingredients:

- 1 tablespoon olive oil
- ½ cup quinoa, rinsed
- 3 cups chicken stock
- 1 pound chicken breast, skinless, boneless and cubed
- ½ teaspoon cumin, ground
- 1 red onion, chopped
- 4 garlic cloves, minced
- ½ teaspoon turmeric powder
- A pinch of salt and black pepper
- 1 teaspoon lemon juice

Directions:

1. Set the instant pot on sauté mode, add the oil, heat it up, add the meat, onion, garlic, turmeric and cumin, toss and brown for 5 minutes.
2. Add the remaining ingredients, put the lid on and cook on High for 15 minutes.
3. Release the pressure fast for 6 minutes, stir the stew, divide it into bowls and serve.

Nutritional Values per serving: Calories 200, fat 12, fiber 4, carbs 7, protein 14

Light Lunch Soup

Preparation Time: 43 MINS

Serving: 6

Ingredients

- 1 tbsp. olive oil
- 1 chopped yellow onion
- 3 minced garlic cloves
- 1¼ pounds frozen cauliflower
- ½ pound cubed frozen butternut squash
- 3 cups filtered water
- 1 tsp dried thyme
- 1 tsp paprika
- ½ tsp red pepper flakes
- Salt, to taste
- ½ cup half-and-half
- ¼ cup shredded cheddar cheese

Directions:

1. Place the oil in the Instant Pot and select "Sauté". Then add the onion and cook for about 4-5 minutes.
2. Add garlic and cook for about 1 minute.
3. Select the "Cancel" and stir in cauliflower, squash, water, thyme and spices.
4. Secure the lid and place the pressure valve to "Seal" position.
5. Select "Manual" and cook under "High Pressure" for about 5 minutes.
6. Select the "Cancel" and carefully do a "Quick" release.
7. Remove the lid and stir in half-and-half.
8. With an immersion blender, puree the soup and serve immediately.

Nutritional Values per serving:

Calories 117

Total Fat 6.5g

Net Carbs 2.16g

Protein 4.4g

Fiber 3.8g

North-American Veggie Soup

Preparation Time: 38 MINS

Serving: 6

Ingredients:

- 2 tsp olive oil
- 1 chopped small yellow onion
- 1 tbsp. minced garlic
- 1 tsp dried thyme
- 1 pound chopped fresh Baby Bella mushrooms
- 4 cups chopped cauliflower
- 6 cups homemade vegetable broth
- ¾ cup grated Parmesan cheese

Directions:

1. Place the oil in the Instant Pot and select "Sauté". Then add the onion and garlic and cook for about 2-3 minutes.
2. Add mushrooms and cook for about 4-5 minutes.
3. Select the "Cancel" and stir in cauliflower and broth.
4. Secure the lid and place the pressure valve to "Seal" position.
5. Select "Manual" and cook under "High Pressure" for about 5 minutes.
6. Select the "Cancel" and carefully do a Natural release.

7. Remove the lid and with an immersion blender, puree the soup.
8. Select the "Sauté" and stir in Parmesan cheese.
9. Cook for about 5 minutes.
10. Serve immediately.

Nutritional Values per serving:

Calories 147

Total Fat 69g

Net Carbs 1.5g

Protein 13.8g

Fiber 2.6g

Bolognese Soup

Preparation Time: 40 MIN

Serving: 4

Ingredients:

- 1 pound ground Beef
- 14 ounces diced canned Tomatoes
- ¼ cup Tomato Puree
- 3 cups Chicken Broth
- ½ tsp Thyme
- ½ tsp Oregano
- 1 tbsp. chopped Basil
- 2 Garlic Cloves, minced
- 2 cups Cauliflower Rice
- ½ tsp Sweetener
- ½ tsp Salt
- ½ tsp Pepper
- 1 tbsp. Olive Oil

Directions:

1. Heat the oil in your IP on SAUTE.
2. Add onions and cook for 3 minutes.
3. Add garlic, oregano, and thyme, and cook for 1 more minute.
4. Add the beef and cook until browned.
5. Stir in the tomato puree and tomatoes, and cook for 2 more minutes.
6. Pour the broth over.
7. Add salt, pepper, and sweetener, and close the lid.
8. Cook on HIGH for 5 minutes.
9. Let the pressure drop for 5 minutes.
10. Stir in the cauliflower and cook for 5 more minutes on HIGH.
11. Release the pressure naturally.
12. Stir in the basil and serve.
13. Enjoy!

Nutritional Values per serving:

Calories 423

Total Fats 17.4g

Net Carbs 7g

Protein 25g

Fiber: 1.8g

Ham and Asparagus Soup

Preparation Time: 55 MIN

Serving: 4

Ingredients:

- 1 ½ pounds Asparagus Split, chopped
- ½ tsp Thyme
- ¾ cup diced Ham
- 1 Onion, diced
- 3 tbsp. Ghee
- 2 tsp minced Garlic
- 4 cups Chicken Broth

Directions:

1. Melt the ghee in your IP on SAUTE.
2. Add onions and cook for 3 minutes.
3. Add ham and garlic and cook for 1 more minute.
4. Add the thyme and broth and stir to combine.
5. Close the lid and cook on SOUP for 45 minutes.
6. Release the pressure quickly.
7. Blend with a hand blender until smooth.
8. Serve and enjoy!

Nutritional Values per serving:

Calories 233

Total Fats 18.5g

Net Carbs 7.5g

Protein 8.7g

Fiber: 2.6g

A Different Wedding Soup

Preparation Time: 45 MIN

Serving: 4

Ingredients:

- 3 cups Bone Broth
- 4 ounces Spinach
- ½ Onion, chopped
- 1 cup diced Ham
- ½ tsp Turmeric
- ½ tsp Garlic Powder
- ½ cup chopped Celery
- 1 Carrot, sliced thinly
- 1 tsp Thyme
- 1 cup Cauliflower Rice
- Meatballs:
- 1/2 pound ground Beef
- 1 tbsp. Almond Flour
- ½ tsp Oregano
- ½ tsp Parsley
- ¼ tsp Pepper

Directions:

1. In a bowl, mix all of the meatball ingredients.
2. Shape into meatballs.
3. Place all of the remaining ingredients, except the ham, in your Instant Pot and stir to combine.
4. Add the meatballs and lock the lid.
5. Cook on SOUP for 30 minutes.
6. Release the pressure naturally.
7. Stir in the ham and serve.
8. Enjoy!

Nutritional Values per serving:

Calories 180

Total Fats 8g

Net Carbs 4.7

Protein 22g

Fiber: 3.5g

Oxtail Soup

Preparation Time: 4 hours

Serving: 8

Ingredients:

- 3 ½ pounds Oxtails
- 3 Bay Leaves
- 1 Celery Stalks, chopped
- 2 cups Green Beans
- 1 Rutabaga, diced
- 14 ounces canned diced Tomatoes
- ¼ cup Ghee
- 1 Thyme Sprig
- 1 Rosemary Sprig
- 2 Leeks, sliced
- 2 ½ quarts Water
- 2 tbsp. Lemon Juice
- ¼ tsp ground Cloves
- Salt and Pepper, to taste

Directions:

1. Melt the ghee in your IP on SAUTE.
2. Add the oxtails and cook until browned. You may need to work in batches here.

3. Pour the water over and add the thyme rosemary, bay leaves, and cloves.
4. Cook on HIGH for 1 hour.
5. Do a natural pressure release.
6. Remove the meat from the IP and shred on a cutting board.
7. Add the rutabaga and leeks to the pot and close the lid.
8. Cook on HIGH for 5 minutes.
9. Add the remaining veggies and cook for 7 minutes more.
10. Add the meat and close again.
11. Cook on HIGH for 2 minutes.
12. Stir in the lemon juice and season with salt and pepper.
13. Serve and enjoy!

Nutritional Values per serving:

Calories 371

Total Fats 22g

Net Carbs 8.2g

Protein 33g

Fiber: 2.7g

Taco Soup

Preparation Time: 25 MIN

Serving: 8

Ingredients:

- 1 lbs Ground Pork
- 1 lbs Ground Beef
- 16 oz Cream Cheese
- 20 oz Ro-Tel Diced Tomatoes and Green Chilies
- 2 tbsp. Taco Seasonings
- 4 cups Chicken Broth
- 2 tbsp. Coriander Leaves (chopped
- ½ cup Monterey Jack (grated

Directions:

1. Set the Instant Pot to "Saute" and place in it the ground meats. Cook while frequently stirring and breaking larger chunks until all water has evaporated, some 10 minutes.
2. Add the cream cheese, Ro-Tel and taco seasonings, and stir well to combine.
3. Place and lock the lid and manually set cooking time to 15 minutes at high pressure.
4. When done quick release the pressure. Stir in the coriander leaves.

5. Serve topped with the grated Monterey Jack.

Nutritional Values per serving:

Calories: 547

Total Fats: 43g

Net Carbs: 4g

Proteins: 33g

Fibers: 1g

Minestrone Soup

Preparation Time: 35 MIN

Serving: 12

Ingredient S:

- 2 tbsp. Olive Oil
- 1 Sweet Potato (diced
- 1 cup Carrots (diced
- 2 stalks Celery (diced
- 2 medium Zucchini (diced
- 2 medium Shallots (diced
- 2 cloves Garlic (minced
- 28 oz Chicken Broth
- 28 oz Tomatoes (diced
- 1 cup Fresh Spinach (chopped
- 2 Bay Leaves
- 2 tsp Dried Oregano
- 1 tsp Dried Basil
- 1 tsp Dried Parsley
- ½ tsp Cayenne Pepper
- ½ tsp Salt
- 1 tsp Ground Black Pepper
- 1½ lbs Ground Pork Sausage (cooked and crumbled)

Directions:

1. Pour olive oil in the Instant Pot. Add all the other ingredients, except spinach, to the pot and stir to combine.
2. Place and lock the lid and set the Instant Pot to "Soup" or manually to 30 minutes cooking time at high pressure.
3. When done quick release the pressure.
4. Remove the bay leaf, and add the spinach to the pot, stir and let sit for 2-3 minutes until wilted.
5. Serve warm.

Nutritional Values per serving:

Calories: 254

Total Fats: 18g

Net Carbs: 8g

Proteins: 11g

Fibers: 2g

Coconut Tomato Soup

Preparation Time: 10 MIN

Serving: 4

Ingredients:

- 1 can Coconut Milk
- 1 medium Red Onion (diced
- 6 Roma Tomatoes (quartered
- ¼ cup Coriander Leaves (chopped
- 1 tsp Garlic (minced
- 1 tsp Ginger (minced
- 1 tsp Salt
- ½ tsp Cayenne Pepper
- 1 tsp Turmeric
- 1 tbsp. Agave Nectar

Directions:

1. Place all ingredients in the Instant Pot and stir to combine.
2. Place and lock the lid, and manually set the cooking time to 5 minutes at high pressure.
3. Let naturally release the pressure for 10 minutes and then quick release it.
4. With a hand blender blend the soup until smooth.
5. Serve warm.

Nutritional Values per serving:

Calories: 157

Total Fats: 12g

Net Carbs: 10g

Proteins: 2g

Fibers: 2g

Creamy Chicken Soup

Preparation Time: 10 MIN

Serving: 4

Ingredients:

- 1 medium Onion
- 6 cloves Garlic
- 1 oz Ginger
- 1 cup Coconut Milk
- 10 oz Ro-Tel Canned Tomato and Chilies
- 1 tbsp. Powdered Chicken Broth Base
- 1 tsp Ground Turmeric
- 1 lbs Boneless Chicken Thighs (cut into 1½ inch chunks)
- 1½ cups Celery Stalks (chopped)
- 2 cups Swiss Chard (chopped)

Directions:

1. Place the onion, garlic, ginger, tomatoes and chilies, turmeric, broth base, and a half cup of coconut milk in a food processor and blend until smooth.
2. Transfer into the Instant Pot, and add chicken, celery and Swiss chard.
3. Place and lock the lid and manually set the cooking time to 5 minutes at high pressure.

4. When done let the pressure naturally releases for 10 minutes and then quick release it.
5. Add the remaining half cup of coconut milk, stir and serve.

Nutritional Values per serving:

Calories: 405

Total Fats: 31g

Net Carbs: 9g

Proteins: 21g

Fibers: 2g

Ham and Bean Soup

Preparation Time: 35 MIN

Serving: 6

Ingredients:

- 1 cup Dried Black Soybeans (soaked overnight and drained
- 1 cup Onion (diced
- 1 cup Celery Stalks (diced
- 4 cloves Garlic (minced
- 1 tsp Dried Oregano
- 1 tsp Salt
- 1 tsp Cajun Seasoning
- 1 tsp Liquid Smoke
- 2 tsp Tony Chachere's All Purpose Seasoning
- 1 tsp Louisiana Hot Sauce
- 2 Ham Hocks
- 2 cups Ham (diced
- 2 cups Water

Directions:

1. Place all ingredients in the Instant Pot and stir to combine.
2. Place and lock the lid, and manually set cooking time to 30 minutes at high pressure.

3. When done let pressure releases naturally for 10 minutes and then quick release it.
4. Remove the meat from bone and shred all meat, discarding the bones.
5. Stir to combine, and serve hot.

Nutritional Values per serving:

Calories: 269

Total Fats: 14g

Net Carbs: 10g

Proteins: 21g

Fibers: 3g

Chicken Mushroom Soup

Preparation Time: 10 MIN

Serving: 4

Ingredients:

- 1 medium Onion (cut into thin ribs
- 3 cloves Garlic (minced
- 2 cups Mushrooms (sliced
- 1 small Yellow Squash (chopped
- 1 lbs Chicken Breast (skinless, cut into 2-inch chunks
- 2½ cups Chicken Broth
- 1 tsp Salt
- 1 tsp Ground Black Pepper
- 1 tsp Italian Seasoning

Directions:

1. Place all ingredients in the Instant Pot.
2. Place and lock the lid, and manually set the cooking time to 15 minutes at high pressure.
3. When done let naturally release the pressure for 10 minutes and then quick release it.
4. Remove the chicken from pot, and using a hand blender roughly puree the vegetables.
5. Shred the chicken with a fork and return to pot.
6. Stir to combine and serve.

Nutritional Values per serving:

Calories: 289

Total Fats: 15g

Net Carbs: 8g

Proteins: 30g

Fibers: 1g

Chicken Kale Soup

Preparation Time: 5 MIN

Serving: 4

Ingredients:

- 2 cups Chicken Breast (cooked
- 12 oz Kale (frozen
- 1 medium Onion (diced
- 4 cups Chicken Broth
- ½ tsp Cinnamon
- 1 pinch Ground Cloves
- 2 tsp Garlic (minced
- 1 tsp Ground Black Pepper
- 1 tsp Salt

Directions:

1. Place all ingredients in the Instant Pot.
2. Place and lock the lid and manually set the cooking time to 5 minutes at high pressure.
3. When done let naturally release the pressure for 10 minutes and then quick release it.
4. Adjust the seasonings if needed and serve warm.

Nutritional Values per serving:

Calories: 143

Total Fats: 2g

Net Carbs: 4g

Proteins: 23g

Fibers: 0g

Italian Sausage Kale Soup

Preparation Time: 5 MIN

Serving: 6

Ingredients:

- 1 lbs Hot Italian Sausage Stuffing
- 1 cup Onion diced
- 6 cloves Garlic minced
- 12 oz Cauliflower frozen
- 12 oz Kale frozen
- 3 cups Water
- ½ cup Heavy Cream
- ½ cup Parmesan Cheese grated

Directions:

1. Set the Instant Pot to "Saute"
2. Turn your pressure cooker on to Sauté. Add in the Italian sausage stuffing and lightly brown, while constantly stirring to break the chunks, for 2 minutes.
3. Add the onions and garlic, and mix well to combine.
4. Add the cauliflower, kale and three cups of water.
5. Place and lock the lid, and manually set cooking time to 3 minutes at high pressure.
6. When done let naturally release the pressure and then quick release it.

7. Slowly stir in the cream.
8. Serve sprinkled with parmesan.

Nutritional Values per serving:

Calories: 400

Total Fats: 33g

Net Carbs: 7g

Proteins: 16g

Fibers: 1g

Chickpea Soup with Greens

Preparation Time: 6 MIN

Serving: 6

Ingredients:

- 4 cups Leeks (thinly sliced
- 1 cup Celery Stalks (sliced
- 15 oz Chickpeas (canned
- 8 cups Rainbow Chard (chopped
- 1 tbsp. Garlic (minced
- 1 tsp Dried Oregano
- 1 tsp Salt
- 2 tsp Ground Black Pepper
- 2 cups Vegetable Stock
- 2 cups Straightneck Squash (cut into 1-inch cubes)
- ¼ cup Parsley (chopped)
- 6 tbsp. Parmesan Cheese (grated)

Directions:

1. Place into the Instant Pot the leeks, celery, chickpeas, chard, garlic, oregano, salt, pepper and vegetable stock. Stir to combine.
2. Place and lock the lid, and manually set the cooking time to 3 minutes at high pressure.
3. When done quick release the pressure.

4. Set the Instant Pot to "Saute" and add the squash and parsley. Stir to combine and cook 3 more minutes.
5. Serve sprinkled with parmesan.

Nutritional Values per serving:

Calories: 142

Total Fats: 14g

Net Carbs: 14g

Proteins: 6g

Fibers: 5g

Cheesy Meatball Soup

Preparation Time: 5-10 MIN

Serving: 12

Ingredients:

- 1 lbs Lean Ground Beef
- 1 Egg
- ¼ cup LC Breading & Crusting Mix
- 1 tsp Salt
- 1 tsp Oregano
- 1 tbsp. Parsleychopped
- ½ tsp Garlic Powder
- ½ tsp Ground Black Pepper
- For the stock
- 2 cups Beef Broth
- ½ medium Green Bell Pepper diced
- ½ medium Red Bell Pepper diced
- 1 stalk Celery diced
- ½ cup Red Onion diced
- 5 large Mushrooms diced
- Cheese Sauce:
- 4 tbsp. Water
- 4 tbsp. Heavy Cream
- 4 tbsp. Butter

- 8 slices American Cheese

Directions:

1. Place in a bowl the beef, egg, breading mixture, salt, oregano, parsley, garlic and pepper, and mix well to combine. Form into 2 inch balls and set aside.
2. Place in the Instant Pot the beef broth, green and red peppers, celery, onions and mushrooms, and stir to combine.
3. Place the meatballs in broth.
4. Place and lock the lid, and manually set the cooking time to 10 minutes.
5. When there is 3 minutes left on the timer, combine in a microwave safe bowl the water, cream, butter and American cheese.
6. Microwave the cheese sauce for 2-3 minutes until blended, stirring every 30 seconds.
7. Quick release the pressure and stir in the cheese sauce.
8. Serve warm.

Nutritional Values per serving:

Calories: 419

Total Fats: 32g

Net Carbs: 3.7g

Proteins: 27g

Fibers: 2g

Clam Chowder

Preparation Time: 15 MIN

Serving: 8

Ingredients:

- 16 rashers Bacon diced
- 1 cup Onion (diced
- 1 cup Celery Stalks diced
- 2 cans Fancy Whole Baby Clams
- 2 cups Chicken Broth
- 2 cups Heavy Cream
- 1 tsp Thyme
- 1 tsp Salt
- 1 tsp Ground Black Pepper

Directions:

1. Set the Instant Pot to "Saute" and add to it bacon. Cook until crispy, some 6-7 minutes.
2. Add the onion and celery and saute until soft some 2-3 minutes, while occasionally stirring.
3. Add all the rest of ingredients and stir to combine.
4. Place and lock the lid and manually set the cooking time to 5 minutes at high pressure.
5. When done quick release the pressure.
6. Serve warm.

Nutritional Values per serving:

Calories: 427

Total Fats: 33g

Net Carbs: 5g

Proteins: 27g

Fibers: 0g

Sausage Bacon and Mushroom Chowder

Preparation Time: 5-10 MIN

Serving: 14

Ingredients:

- 4 cups Chicken Broth
- 2 cups Heavy Cream
- 2 cups Mushrooms (sliced
- 2 cups Ground Sausage (cooked
- 6 rashers Bacon (fried and crumbled
- 1 cup Daikon Radish (diced
- ½ cup Onion (diced
- ½ cup Red Bell Pepper (diced
- ½ cup Parmesan Cheese
- 1 tbsp. Dried Parsley Leaves
- 1 tsp Garlic Powder
- 1 tsp Salt
- 1 tsp Ground Black Pepper
- ½ tsp Thyme

Directions:

1. Place all ingredients in the Instant Pot.
2. Place and lock the lid and manually set the cooking time to 5 minutes at high pressure.
3. When done quick release the pressure.
4. Serve warm.

Nutritional Values per serving:

Calories: 316

Total Fats: 33g

Net Carbs: 3g

Proteins: 14g

Fibers: 1g

Turkey and Daikon Chowder

Preparation Time: 5-10 MIN

Serving: 12

Ingredients:

- 1 lbs Lean Ground Turkey (cooked, drained and crumbled
- 3 cups Daikon Radish (diced
- 10 cups Chicken Broth
- 2 cups Heavy Cream
- 2 cups Mozzarella (shredded
- 4 cups Antipasto Trail Mix
- 1 tbsp. Dried Parsley Leaves
- 1 tbsp. Dried Chives
- 1 tsp Salt
- 1 tsp Ground Black Pepper
- 1 tsp Garlic Powder

Directions:

1. Place all ingredients in the Instant Pot.
2. Place and lock the lid and manually set the cooking time to 5 minutes at high pressure.
3. When done quick release the pressure.
4. Serve warm.

Nutritional Values per serving:

Calories: 232

Total Fats: 9.1g

Net Carbs: 5.1g

Proteins: 13.2g

Fibers: 2.4g

Pork and Vegetable Stock Recipe

Preparation Time:: 66 minutes

Servings: 8

Ingredients:

- 2 lb. pastured pork bones
- 1/2 cup carrots; chopped.
- 1/2 cup bell peppers
- 1/2 tsp. whole black peppercorns
- 8 cups water
- 1 tsp. dried bay leaf
- 1 sprig fresh parsley
- 1/2 cup green onions; chopped.
- 1 celery stalk; chopped into thirds
- 1 small onion; unpeeled and halved
- 1 tsp. kosher salt

Directions:

1. Pour the water into the instant pot.
2. Add all the Ingredients to the water. Close the instant pot lid and turn the pressure release handle to the *sealed* position.
3. Select the *Manual* function; set to high pressure and adjust the timer to 20 minutes

4. When it beeps; *Natural Release* the steam for 10 minutes and open the instant pot lid
5. Strain the prepared stock through a mesh strainer and discard all the solids, Skim off all the surface fats and serve hot.

Chicken Stock Recipe

Preparation Time: 66 minutes

Servings: 8

Ingredients:

- 2½ lb. chicken carcass
- 1/2 tsp. whole black peppercorns
- 10 cups water
- 1 sprig fresh parsley
- 1 celery stalk; chopped into thirds
- 1 small onion; unpeeled and halved
- 1 tsp. dried bay leaf
- 1 tsp. kosher salt

Directions:

1. Pour the water into the instant pot.
2. Add all the Ingredients to the water
3. Secure the lid. Turn the pressure release handle to the *sealed* position.
4. Select the *Manual* function. Set to high pressure and adjust the time to 60 minutes
5. When it beeps; *Natural Release* the steam for 10 minutes and open the instant pot lid.
6. Strain the prepared stock through a mesh strainer and discard all the solids, Skim off all the surface fats and serve hot.

www.ingramcontent.com/pod-product-compliance
Lightning Source LLC
Chambersburg PA
CBHW071823080526
44589CB00012B/894